URA

URA Yves Malysse Kiki Verbeeck

A+ Architecture in Belgium
BOZAR Books
Koenig Books

Contents

Foreword

Helen Thomas

Not long ago, I visited the village of Nazareth in the surroundings of Ghent and met the mayor outside the district's new gymnasium and youth centre, completed by URA Yves Malysse Kiki Verbeek in 2018. We gazed at the elegant ensemble of structures before us. 'It's a perfect strategy', the mayor said. 'Everything is drawn together by a single belt and yet opened up, it was easy to choose our winner.' This simple statement alludes to the special qualities of URA's work – its spatial, material and strategic clarity, and its almost-familiar form-making blooming into pared-down theatricality – articulated not by a fellow architect or a critic, but with precious emphasis by a client who is also a close observer and user of the building. As with a vast majority of URA's projects, the commission was the product of a competition system for public buildings initiated in 1999. Making room for the work of new and young practices and overseen by the Flemish Government Architect, this has engendered a rich and vital architectural culture, within which URA's presence has been constant since their first project, a multipurpose hall in Eeklo, which was completed in 2003.

Seen from the outside, Belgium has two scales: one defined by the national boundary, the other by the edges of the city of Brussels – a centre of Europe, both symbolically and physically. The intertwining courses of Belgium's ring roads form Europe's northern crossroads and the heterogeneity of their voyagers hints at a cultural and political complexity that only becomes apparent upon closer inspection. Within these circumstances, URA have situated themselves as Brussels-based architects. This means that they operate from within the overlap between Flanders and Wallonia, living and working in a place that embodies the dialectical qualities that they claim for their own work. In this potential hiatus between the sometimes conflicting realities of Belgium's two halves, URA can benefit from the cross-pollination of their fallout. At the same time, the relative freedom of distance creates a space within which an autonomous synthesis – what they call a contemporary abstract identity – can be conceptualized, and which to achieve they have developed their double-edged approach to site and programme.

Radiating out from the relatively dense heart of Brussels is the wider field of URA's architectural manoeuvres: the nebular city, or the ubiquitous low-density construction that covers the landscape of Flanders in thin lines that follow its criss-crossing networks of roads and streets. Almost all of the 20 projects that are included in this publication belong within this context, but each one maintains its own distinct character that emerges out of URA's lived analysis of the spatial context. Alongside this, they introduce the notion of *Gesamtkunstwerk* – in the traditional sense of a continuous designed environment that goes down to the crafted detail of furniture and specially made joinery – which, incidentally, requires excellent relationships with contractors and subcontractors – but also in a more abstract way. They talk of creating scenarios that are the backdrops to life, that embody atmospheres; they are interested in creating friction that offers multiple possibilities for use. In this, the boundaries of URA's buildings are important players. 'A façade is not two-dimensional', they say. 'It is a dynamic action', perhaps created through tampering with the ground, or making pockets of ambiguous space through facets and selective transparency. Whatever the strategy, it has been worked through rigorously in large-scale façade models.

Finally, and reflecting their consummate strategic skills, is the issue of how they name things. In his essay, Christophe Van Gerrewey refers to Vidler's 'Third Typology', that of the city, connecting it to their name, URA, that refers to Ur, the first city, but also to the classification of their projects. Using an abstraction – three letters deriving from unspoken characteristics of the project rather than recognizable identifying names – they sidestep figurative narrative and precedent, and enter the realm of abstract type. Particularizing these universal basic forms is the principal move, a transforming of archetype as it comes into confrontation with visceral, ephemeral, living contexts.

TXT

Christophe Van Gerrewey

KAU

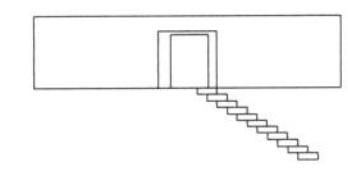

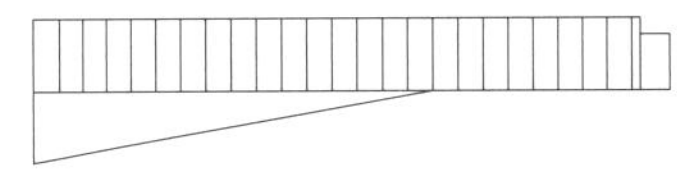

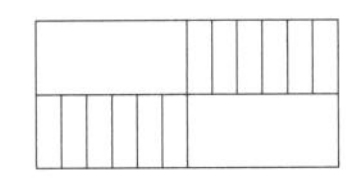

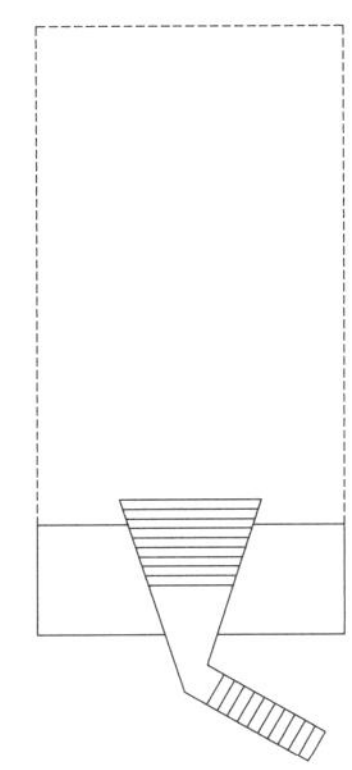

The self-evident quality of URA's architecture is as tranquil as it is deceptive. In the light of the turbulent history of architecture, and of an often neurotic approach to architecture (in Belgium and far beyond), their projects and realizations create a relaxed and carefree impression. This architecture has no more theoretical, political or ideological accounts to settle; history is neither something to break with in the search for the new, nor a canonical reservoir which must be referred to at all costs; and although the position of the architect will always be under discussion, it is precisely that negotiability that does not isolate architecture from the rest of society, for who or what is *not* up for discussion today?

This pragmatic attitude – in the sense that the only truth to which architecture can lay claim lies in the accomplishment of tangible, perceptible and practical changes – is obviously not the privilege of URA. In the 1970s, 1980s and 1990s, 'silent generations' in Belgium produced their work in the margins, not seldom without a justified sense of misunderstanding, and sometimes seeking refuge in more artistic and elated approaches. If URA's generation, which became active around the turn of the century, is 'silent', then that in no way poses a problem. They can afford to remain silent, not because they are forced to, but because they are too busy making architecture. Architecture is the language with which they wish to express themselves, if anything has to be expressed at all. As Geert Bekaert wrote in the book *XX Models: Young Belgian Architecture* (2012), the product of a series of exhibitions and lectures at BOZAR that highlighted a young generation: 'They take part in architecture like others play football. They sometimes have a certain (happy) form of naivety to thank for that freedom to play their own game, but mostly it is the consequence of an intelligent choice.'

Architecture criticism – as a form of football commentary – then seems even more superfluous than usual. However multifaceted or varied, the work speaks for itself: it contains no hidden messages or intentions, and it is best experienced through its use, or in viewing architecture through the many media that enrich life in the twenty-first century. It is precisely for these reasons that criticism – text – remains meaningful, because behind the suppleness with which this 'busy generation' scores one goal after another lie precise and decisive choices that are not always immediately visible – preferences, decisions and forms of knowledge that may not be waiting for translation, but are open to it, if only to make clear what could distinguish URA's work from that of its contemporaries.

The sports hall that URA built in Uccle between 2007 and 2011 is such a collection of effective choices – it is one of their best-known achievements. A beam-shaped volume stands at some distance from a school building. The exceptional character that characterizes PE classes is thus respected, something that would not be the case with an annex. The volume is abstract, to the point of dullness, but this dullness is not given an opportunity to manifest itself – on the one hand owing to the trees and the slopes of the landscape, which frame and 'hold' the building, and on the other hand owing to design decisions, like the entrance hall which, with concrete steps and a sloping porch, marks a beginning (and the beginning of a use), or like the way in which the façade grid remains constant, but with varying materials. Abstraction and recognizability, formality and functionality, context and autonomy: these are contradictions that characterize the work of URA, without unequivocally determining their oeuvre.

RLN

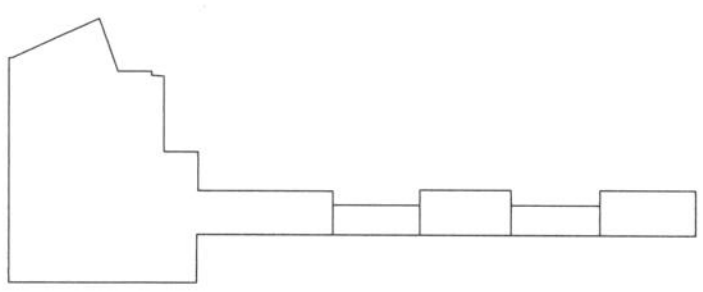

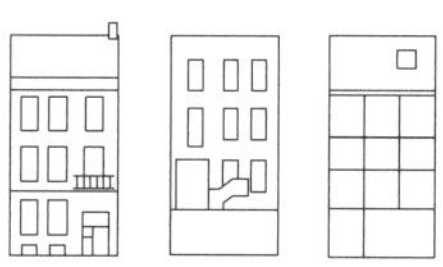

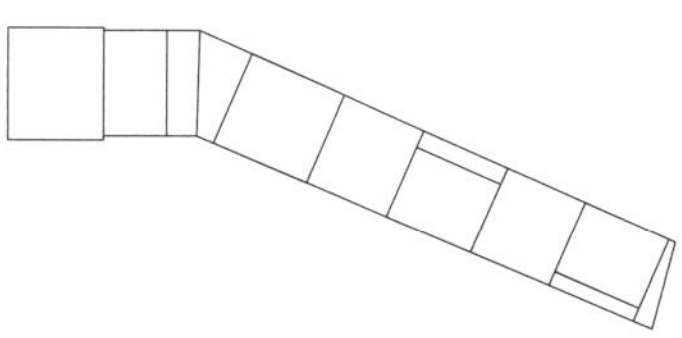

In 2009 URA began an assignment in Ninove, a small town on the outskirts of Brussels: the renovation of a rehabilitation centre for children in a town house that was set for demolition, but whose neoclassical façade is part of a protected cityscape near the station. The station building dated from 1855 and was designed by Jean-Pierre Cluysenaar, who also designed the Galeries Royales Saint-Hubert in Brussels. It was demolished in 1977, a day before it was to be listed, and was replaced by a crushingly gloomy low-rise construction. It outlines Ninove's almost impossible historical context, and the decades of neglect in terms of architecture and urban planning – one of the reasons why the far right won 40 per cent of the vote in 2018.

URA didn't ignore that situation, but didn't worry about it unnecessarily. With their design they show how easy it can be to respect and at the same time transcend an existing urban fabric. The façade was renovated and painted white, and the windows were made as transparent as possible. Behind the façade is a staircase that leads to consultation rooms and that serves to organize a small, bright waiting room on each landing. The back of the front façade is covered with grey slates, like a blind wall. The result resembles a piece of scenery several storeys high – a slightly surprising, but never disturbing element that seems to belong to another world.

The design created for the newly vacant plot illustrates, as other projects do, how URA organizes volumes by first making a fundamental distinction between inside and outside. No matter how small, a building can always benefit from being split up into smaller parts which, thanks to use of materials, sightlines and composition, still form a whole. The front extension of the rehabilitation centre comprises four floors, with the reception and offices on the ground floor and the consultation rooms on the upper storeys. What follows seems to chase the course of a bouncy ball, which first touches the receding volume of the meeting room on the first floor, then lands in the courtyard, bounces over the staff kitchen and reaches the second courtyard – meanwhile veering off to the left, although the pattern of the tiles outside continues straight ahead, unperturbed – and over the small gymnasium, landing in the third courtyard, after which it reaches just enough height to end up, over the doctor's office, on the street that demarcates the plot at the back. In this way, the rehabilitation centre – like every good architectural intervention in a seemingly hopeless context – takes on almost utopian aspirations: it shows how much lighter, happier and better life can be, also in Ninove.

SPP

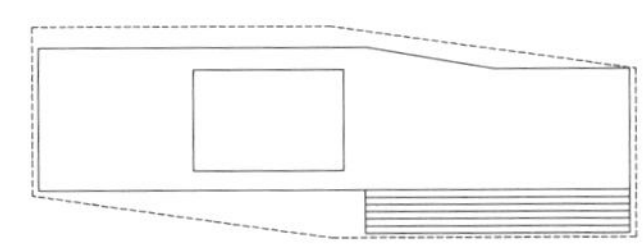

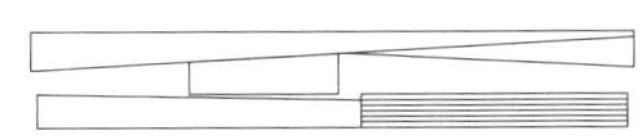

In 1977 Anthony Vidler published a famous essay titled 'The Third Typology' in the magazine *Oppositions*. Since the middle of the eighteenth century, Vidler claimed, there have been two defining typologies in architecture, primary core elements on which the conception of buildings is based. The first typology was the model of the primitive hut, a shelter constructed from branches that magically respected the laws of classicism. The second typology sought models in the industrial production process of building materials and building elements, and led to modernism. The third typology, defined by Vidler, is that of the city, and is thus architectural. Where the first and second typologies confront architecture with an external source – nature or industry – the third typology relies on something that can only come from architecture, because cities simply consist of architecture – squares, walls, façades, columns, roofs and streets. According to Vidler, this third typology belongs neither to classicism nor modernism, but to rationalism.

The question of the fate, after more than 40 years, of the typologies used by Vidler is pertinent. URA's approach is by no means the only one that can help answer this question, but there is something in the office's name already that points in the right direction. In 2007, five years after the founding of URA (with Joost Verstraete as the third founding member), their very first projects were shown in the series *35m³ of Young Architecture* at deSingel in Antwerp. In an interview with Joachim Declerck in the exhibition brochure, Verbeeck said: 'Ur is the name of the first city in the Bible and was also a very deliberate choice for the name of our firm ... We try to recall highly recognizable architectural types, plans and formal idioms.' Malysse added: 'We trust and believe in the qualities to be found in basic types. By confronting them with a new setting, we are able to develop something new with them.'

URA's typological sources are broad, and what they show is that the distinction Vidler made in 1977 is more difficult to make today, especially in the densely built region in which European architects work. In a post-industrial society, the boundaries between nature, industry and the city are largely blurred. What the editors of the Italian magazine *San Rocco* described in 2011 as 'the even covering of the field' is also the condition in which URA works: a chaotic, overcrowded landscape, without patterns, without structures, without clearly definable styles or features. Within this amalgam, is it possible to base a credible typology on natural elements and primary forms of shelter, on industrial and serial production methods, or on an ideal image of the traditional European city? And if so, don't those typologies inevitably involve nostalgic or idealistic reflexes, even more so than 40 years ago?

For example, in the SPP project, a sports hall that URA will build in a sports park in Puurs in 2021, these questions are dismissed as overly theoretical and twentieth-century. The design is based on the archetype of a large, sloping, folded, irregular roof, like an enlarged version of the *shelter* that was built in 2018 on the village square of Watou. Sports areas, changing rooms, a grandstand and a cafeteria will be put to use under this roof, in a clear, functional floor plan whose façades, in the best modernist tradition, are as light as possible. In addition, the building is structured classically and harmoniously, creating vistas, circulation patterns, sightlines and dramatic moments that lend it an urban character. URA's architecture is a controlled mix of the three typologies – or, since it can also be described in this way, uses a fourth, general typology, typical of twenty-first-century architecture, and based on the architecture produced in the twentieth century.

VOS

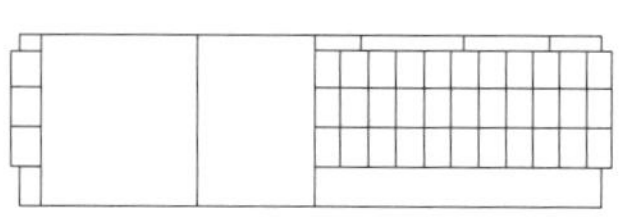

In collaboration with two Belgian offices – Els Claessens and Tania Vandenbussche on the one hand, and Architecten Jan De Vylder Inge Vinck on the other – URA is realizing a housing project in Ghent. It is part of a development bordered by a business park, a hospital, a spaghetti junction, an events complex with an IKEA outlet, a small forest and the Ringvaart, about five minutes by bike from the Gent-Sint-Pieters railway station. Six equally large volumes with a width of 45 metres will be placed against the edge of the forest, on a single line, arranged like the elements of a folding metre; a seventh volume for social housing will be added. On the north side is the Vossenbos, while on the south side is a park whose

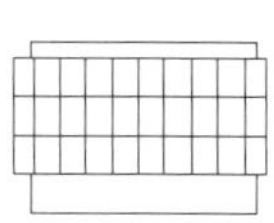

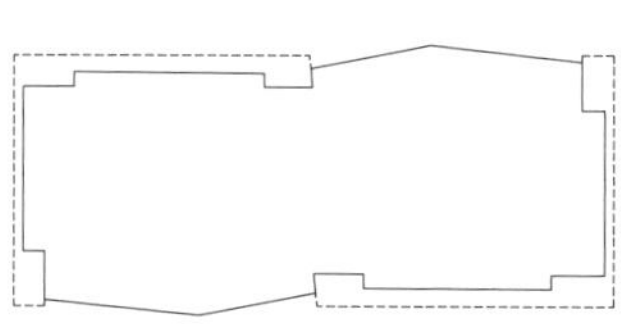

design has been entrusted to Denis Dujardin. It is a bicycle and car park, open on the side of the forest but closed on the side of the park, which connects the six volumes, like the little squares between the buildings, as the hinge points where collective activities take place, but along which access to the dwellings is also organized.

The project makes it possible not only to observe how URA stacks housing typologies and organizes them in part collectively, but also to compare the choices made with those of Belgian contemporaries. The architects have made certain agreements: the building size is identical, as is the number of dwellings per building; all dwellings also have terraces. URA's central decision is to group the terraces and to pack two corners of the building with them, as it were, but in such a way that the building itself is also distorted in function of the terraces. So again, an elementary form – a beam – gets pulled or pushed, without its readability being compromised. The monotony of the minimal and the rudimentary becomes more complex; oppositions are introduced and contrasts increased, but in such a way that a basic tone continues to shimmer through. The same applies to the shell and the window layout: the apartments are not all differentiated from one another (which seems to have become the norm), and yet a completely generic architecture is avoided thanks to differences that manifest themselves on the scale of the building rather than on that of each residential unit.

De Vylder Vinck's strategy is more paradoxical: a floor plan based on a rhythm of parallel strips is combined with a façade in which the same elements are repeated consistently, but in such a detailed and fine-meshed manner that a pointillist impression of complexity and diversity emerges. Of the three collectives in this joint venture, Claessens and Vandenbussche proceed in the most classical way, in that they rely on a façade composition of equally high windows and on terraces and floor plans that are staggered in relation to each other – in contrast to URA, they hold on to the right angle as a compositional principle. Yet the three offices, although using different architectural methods, are looking for the same thing: a grouping of dwellings that does not exclude individuality and variation, but which nevertheless does not have to lead to fragmentation.

WWL

At the back of Leuven railway station, along the Diestsesteenweg, a central workshop of the national railways was set up in 1863, where over the years more than 750 workers would be employed on a nine-hectare site. The walled workshop closed its doors in 1993 and has since slowly been transformed into the new centre of the

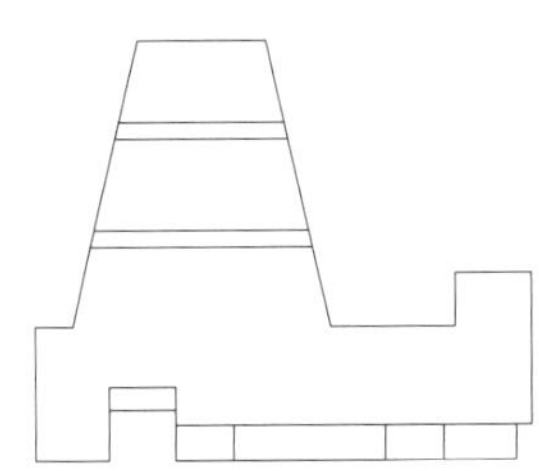

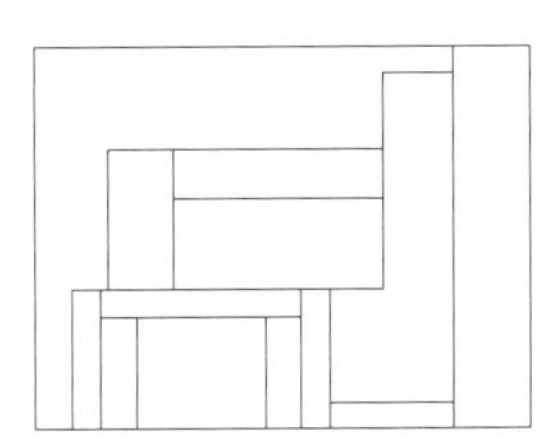

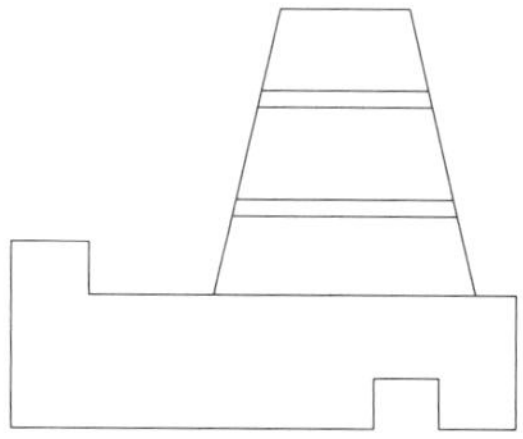

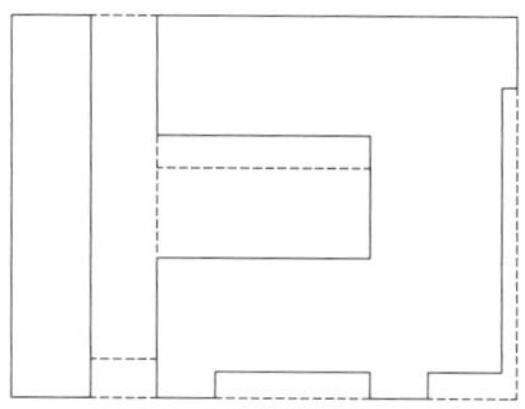

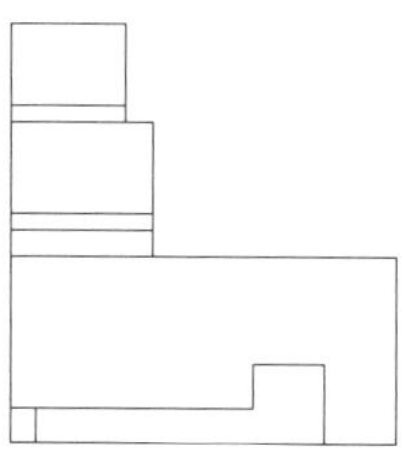

Kessel-Lo district, with public facilities and municipal services, with greenery and squares – and, of course, with housing. On a relatively small part of this site, with a surface area of 2500 m², the city of Leuven decided to realize a residential project – called WWL – for young families with children, for whom market prices in and around the city centre have become too expensive.

The results of the architecture competition were striking. Most submissions adhered to the logic of the city block or proposed variations on it, for example by composing the block out of separate buildings of different heights and with a different layout (De Vylder Vinck), by erecting the four corners of the block to twice the height (Dierendonckblancke), or by leaving one side open, resulting in a semi-public inner area (Happel Cornelisse Verhoeven). URA took a different approach, proposing one large building instead of a block composed of several parts. The result, which will be ready in 2024, consists of a three-storey base filling the entire site, and a single tower volume in a corner that decreases in scope as the height increases. The complex as a whole is uniformly covered with the same natural stone.

The building accommodates a crèche, a music academy, a commercial space for catering and trade, and (in the base) publicly accessible open spaces and play areas. The 48 dwellings are divided into two groups of 20 and 28 units, and each resident group enjoys shared facilities, such as a spare room, outdoor areas, a laundry room, a workplace and a reception room. Housing types include the 'dike house' (located on a play area, with one floor half the size of the other), the bungalow, the urban apartment, the corner house, the winter-garden house, the studio, the house open from front to back, and – mainly at the top – the panorama apartment. What is important is that each unit has its own terrace and that the collective facilities, in accordance with the instructions of the Flemish 'knowledge and expertise centre' Kind en Samenleving (Child and Society), are never further than four floors away from any unit.

The result is a far-reaching alternative to the traditional apartment building, but also to living in a wasteful allotment far removed from public transport and city life. The fact that all the advantages and all the comfort of the suburban dream, which is still ubiquitous in Flanders, are also guaranteed here (thanks to the terraces, the collective spaces, the shared facilities) is not even what matters most. What is more essential, as well as more architectural and symbolic, is the way in which this collective housing takes shape and acquires an important, visible and even monumental presence in Leuven's skyline and cityscape. URA has understood that neither in a post-industrial environment like that of the former central workshops nor in the prepared master plan does it make sense to try to realize classical forms of urbanity – with streets, façades and (nineteenth-century) apartment buildings. Instead, something much larger, more solid and more autonomous will take its place – a building which does not so much 'help build' the city, but which generates its own urbanity – or rather: which articulates what can be understood by urbanity today.

'It seems incredible', Rem Koolhaas wrote in his famous 1993 essay 'Bigness, or the Problem of Large', which was also included in *S,M,L,XL*, 'that the size of a building alone embodies an ideological programme, independent of the will of its architects'. It is indeed the case that buildings of a certain size automatically take on a programmatic and essential character. The remarkable thing about URA's WWL is that this monumentality, this grandeur and self-conscious pride even, is used for an activity that in Belgium has traditionally been organized modestly, hyper-individually, outside the cities and in an utterly fragmentary manner: housing. In the theory and practice of Koolhaas and OMA (and of most other architects), *bigness* is reserved, almost tacitly, for public or corporate programmes, such as libraries and theatres, but also hotels and office buildings. Why in fact do we expect dwellings to dissolve (in the best of cases) in the urban fabric? Why can only public buildings become *fatti urbani*, to use Aldo Rossi's term, by playing a key role in defining the city's image and identity? URA's WWL makes irrefutably visible what cities should be for: to live in.

VKW

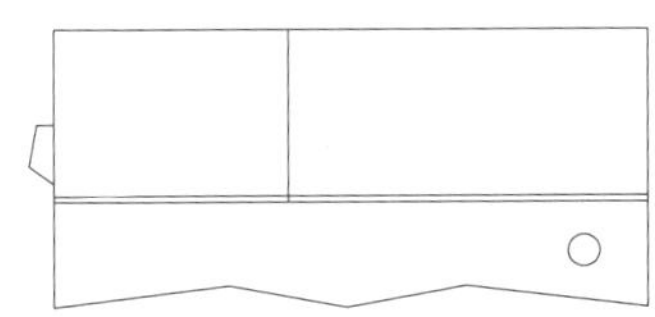

URA has developed a method for cataloguing its own work. Each project is given a name consisting of three block letters (like the name of the office itself), which usually refer to the programme, the client and the location. They also use a number of programmatic categories, such as houses, housing, public, care and infrastructure.

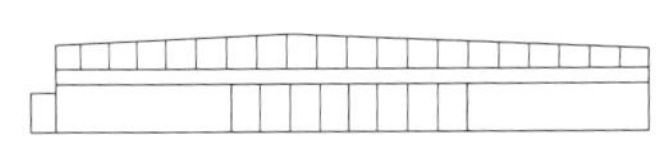

The desire to bring order (by means of language) to the history of architecture in general, or to the production of one office in particular, is inconceivable without historical consciousness and critical self-awareness, and without the need to look back, to look in the mirror or to present oneself in a coherent (and attractive) way to the outside world. The making of architecture cannot be regulated in principle and in advance, although many attempts have been made to do so. The existence of architectural orders is the most literal example: order and theory preceded architecture, as it were; the need to look back or organize did not arise, precisely because buildings were already cataloging themselves in a visible way, like a group of schoolchildren in uniform who line up promptly and obediently. Although it did not prevent many from organizing heroic crusades

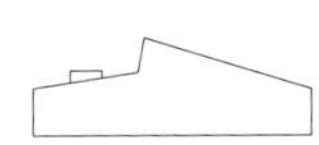

in search of denominators and rules, the idea of a common ground beneath architecture disappeared at the end of the eighteenth and the start of the nineteenth century. It becomes visible in the book compiled by Jean-Nicolas-Louis Durand to chart architectural history in a pseudoscientific and rational way – his 1799 *Recueil et parallèle des édifices de tout genre, anciens et modernes* – as if these were plant species or insects, or in the monograph that Claude-Nicolas Ledoux compiled in 1804 to preserve and organize a small part of his oeuvre, using principles that, ostensibly, lay outside architecture itself: *L'Architecture considérée sous le rapport de l'art, des moeurs et de la législation*. In other words, the big problem is that architecture no longer has its own irrefutable categories. Buildings can be 'sorted', and architects can try to develop an approach or a recognizable style – the associated characteristics are never necessary, they are always up for discussion, and they have to be demonstrated experimentally time and again.

And yet it is impossible to make architecture entirely without shared principles and reliable tools, just as it is impossible to live without certain values and truths, no matter how temporary, imaginary or retroactive those beliefs may be. Such an intuition, of silent knowledge, lies at the basis of URA's classification system, and also gives direction to their work. A final example is a small multipurpose building on the outskirts of the village of Westrozebeke, built in 2019. It overlooks two soccer fields and a patchwork of farmlands, and it accommodates a cafeteria and an after-school childcare centre with a playground. That's all it is: five bays of equal width, which are then bordered by a roof and a façade, both folded idiosyncratically. The result is a building that hardly stands out in this context that can still be called agrarian, because it is subtly reminiscent of non-symmetrical barns, DIY constructions and seemingly self-generated structures. It possesses the same efficiency, clarity and carefreeness, which is why the well-known 'discordant note in the tranquility' – that Adolf Loos, in his 1910 essay 'Architecture', heard every time an architect thought it necessary to bluntly celebrate his or her creativity – does not resonate over there in Westrozebeke. The building is not disturbing, it is where it belongs, and yet it's new, and not invisible, and it makes that place different, prvileged, and better. This opposition between self-evident and new, between invisible and conspicuous, once again suggests that there is an unidentifiable, hidden origin where architecture begins. Each individual building can derive need from it, and the conversation about architecture can rest on it, so that society and architecture remain connected.

Atlas

1. MDA, Master plan campus UA, Antwerp 2. VOS, Housing, Ghent 3. VOS, Housing, Ghent 4. SPP, Sports facilitites, Puurs
5. WWL, Collective housing, Leuven 6. CIX, Housing, Antwerp

1

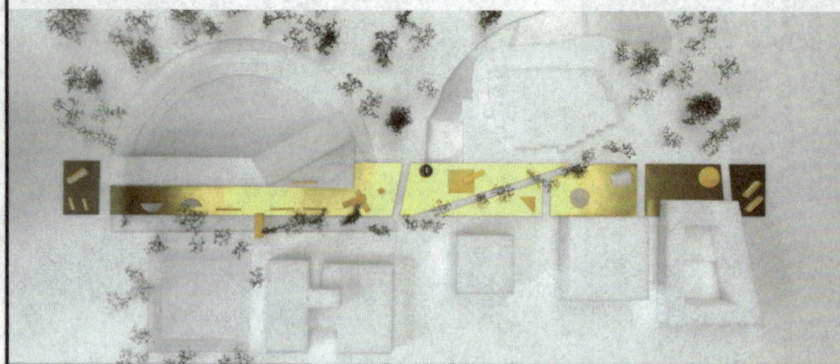

2

3

4

5

6

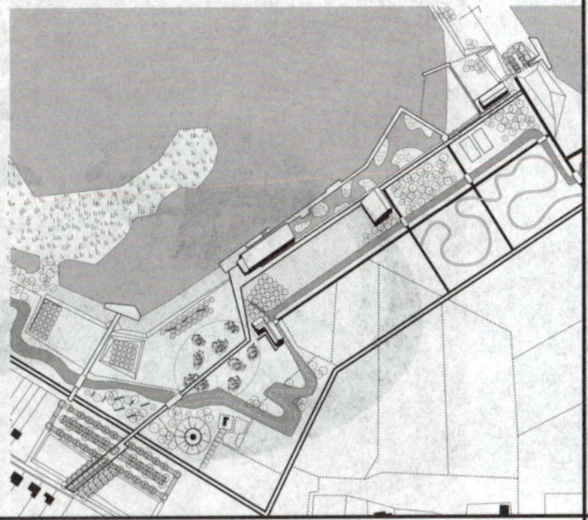

8

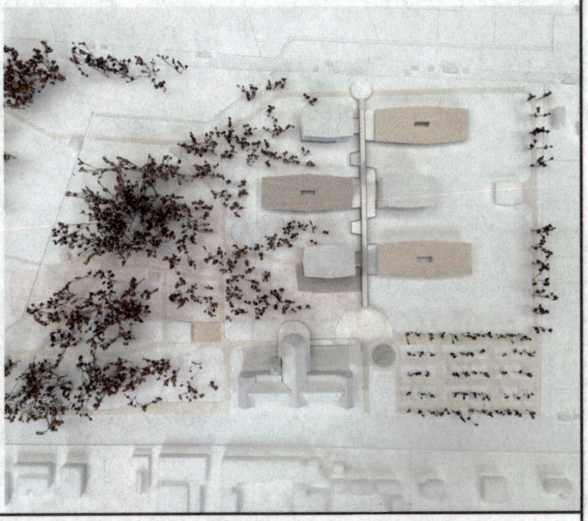

10

11

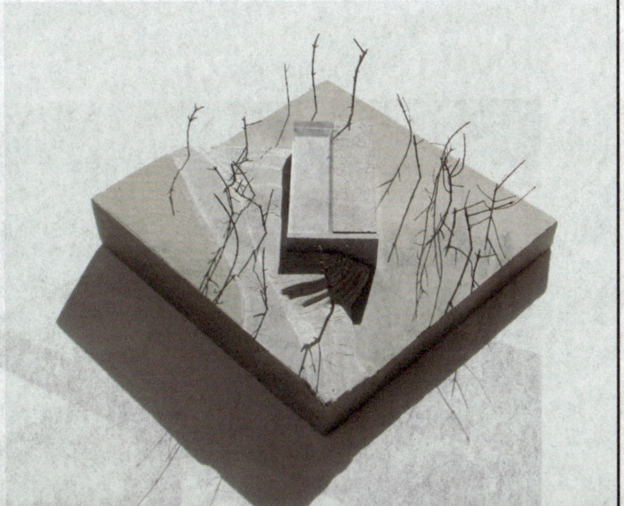

12

7. GAV, Master plan for nature and leisure park, Harelbeke 8. RPZ, Rehabilitation campus, Zandhoven 9. TJN, Gymnasium and youth centre, Nazareth 10. RLN, Rehabilitation centre, Ninove 11. KAU, Gymnasium, Uccle 12. IBB, Reorganization of the Interbeton site, Brussels

1. GWB, Gudule urban winery, Brussels 2. PLM, Botanic garden, Meise 3. IBB, Reorganization of the Interbeton site, Brussels
4. BLB, Bus station, Bruges 5. PLM, Botanic garden, Meise 6. GOD, Conversion concrete power station, Ghent

1

2

3

4

5

6

8

10

1

12

7. DPL, Offices and pavilion, Leuven 8. JDC, House for an artist 9. PLM, Botanic garden, Meise
10. TAH, School, Heist-op-den-Berg 11. VKW, Community centre, Westrozebeke 12. WWL, Collective housing, Leuven

1. THB, Heysel tram terminus, Brussels 2. VOS, Housing, Ghent 3. GOD, Conversion concrete power station, Ghent 4. GCG, Community centre, Geluwe 5. PLM, Botanic Garden, Meise 6. BPB, Mail sorting centre, Brussels

1

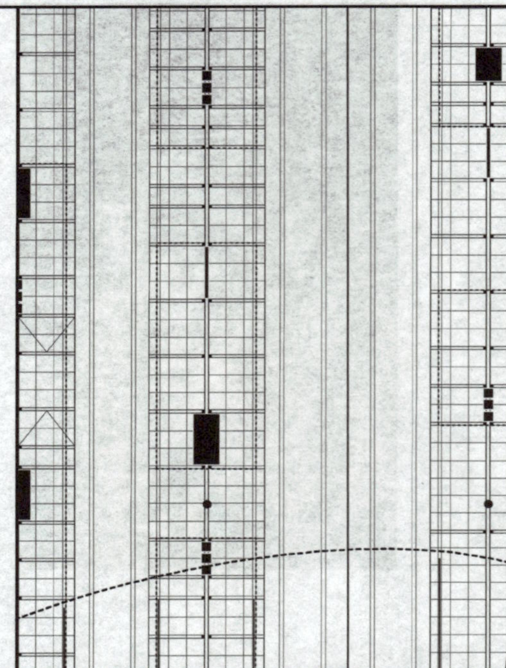

2

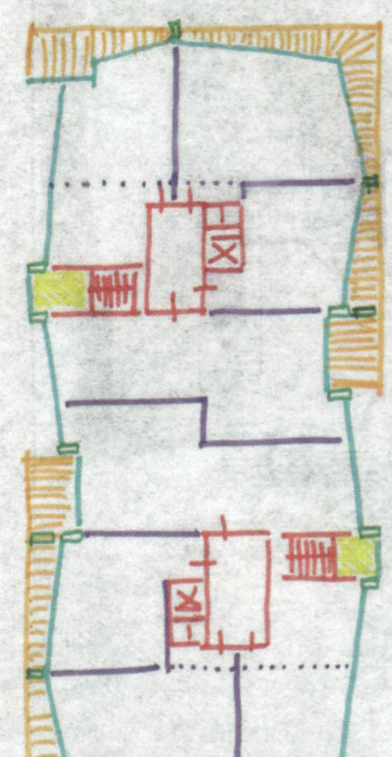

3

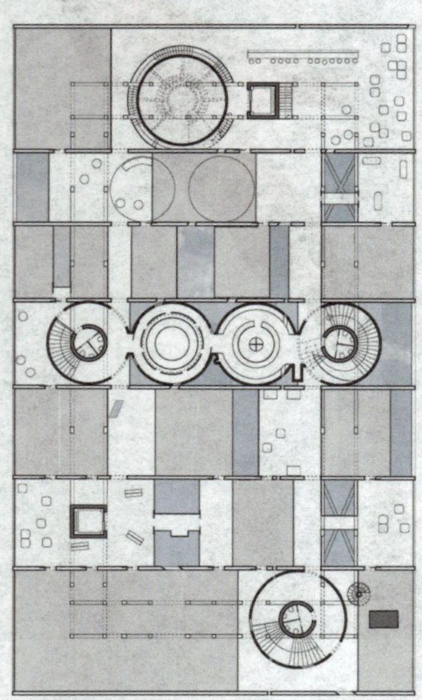

4

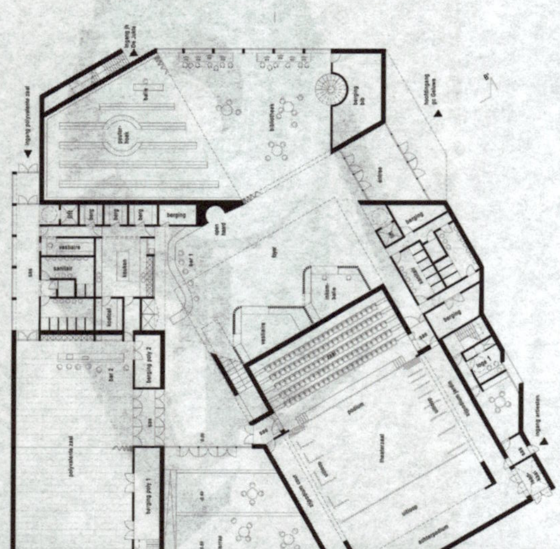

5

6

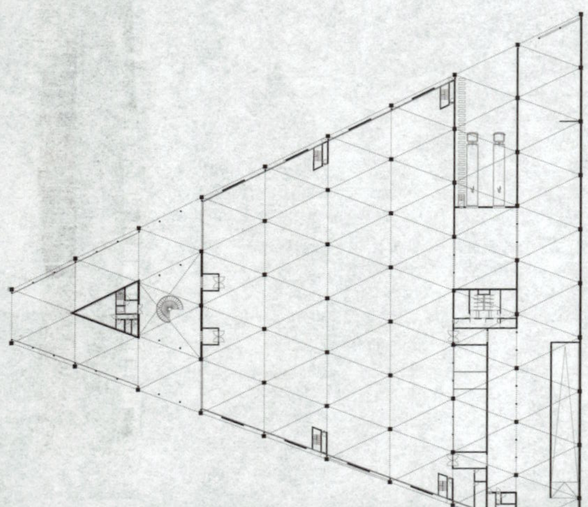

7

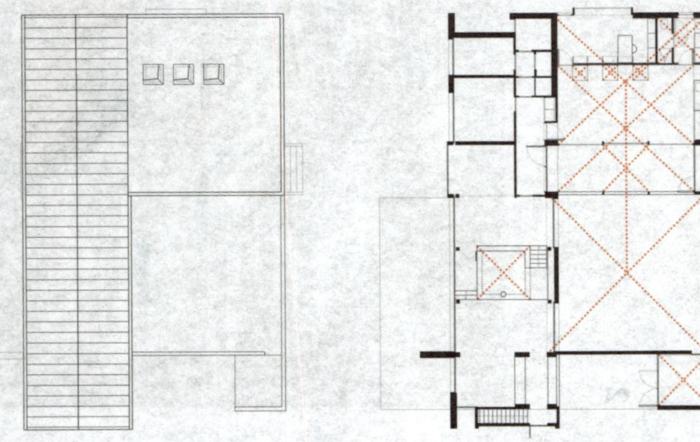

8

9

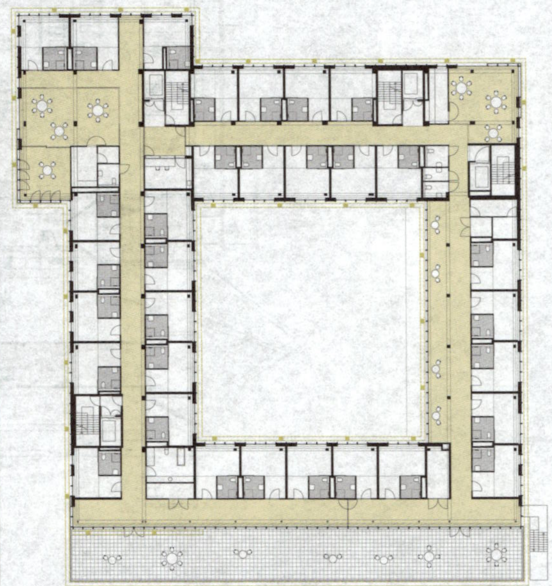

10

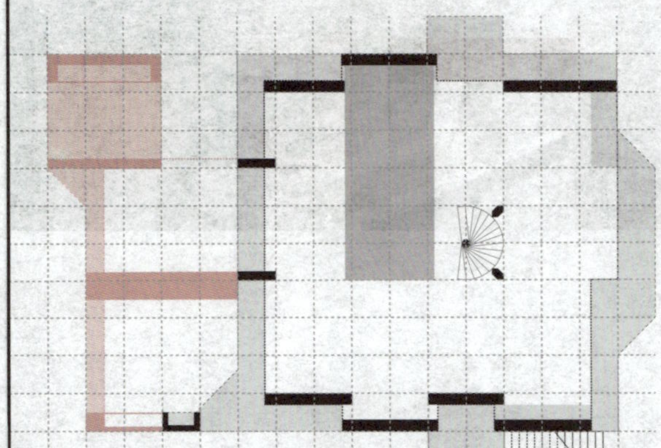

11

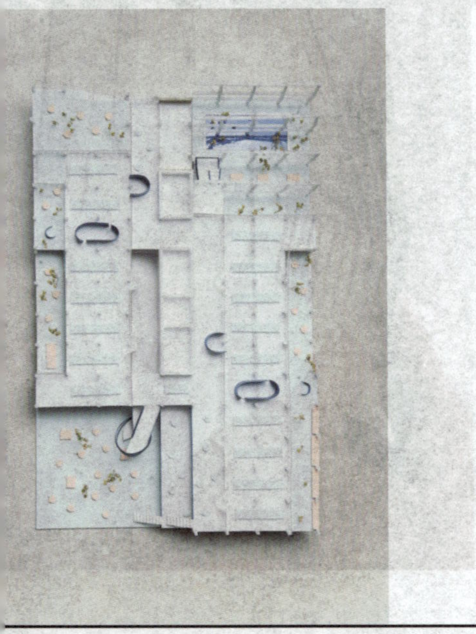

12

7. JKB, Extension single-family house, Beersel 8. PLM, Botanic Garden, Meise 9. WZK, Residential care centre, Kortrijk
10. BVD, Extension single-family house, Dilbeek 11. AQA, Campus Aquafin, Aartselaar 12. FAR, Single-family house, Rumbeke

1. BTL, Kindergarten and primary school, Laeken 2. WFA, Housing, Antwerp 3. BVD, Extension single-family house, Dilbeek
4. GOD, Conversion concrete power station, Ghent 5. VKW, Community centre, Westrozebeke 6. LSN, Boat shed, Nieuwpoort

1

2

3

4

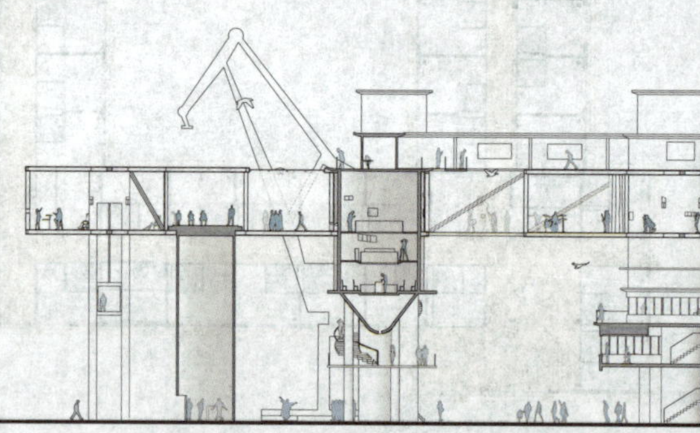

5

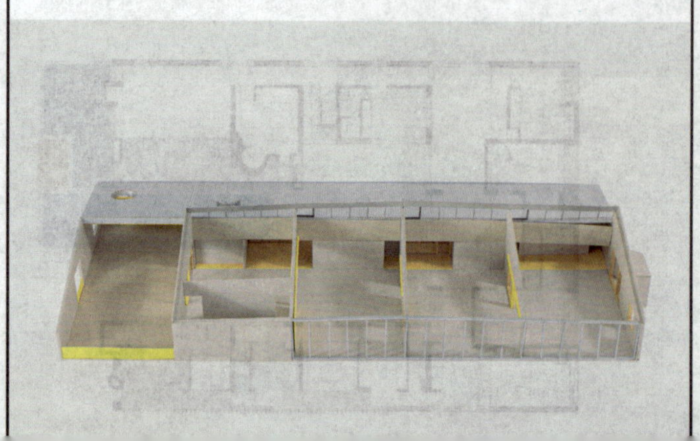

6

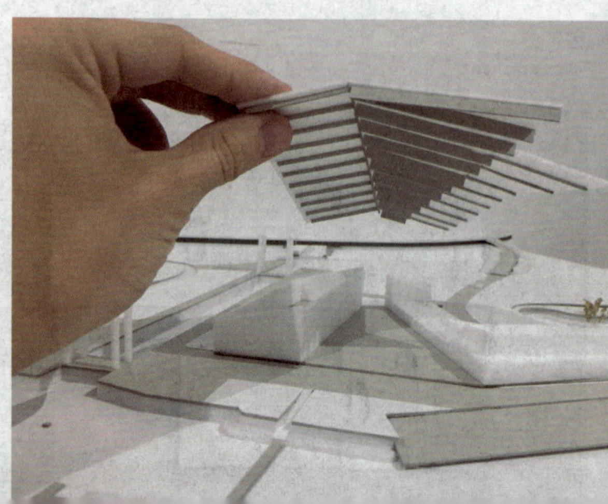

7

8

9

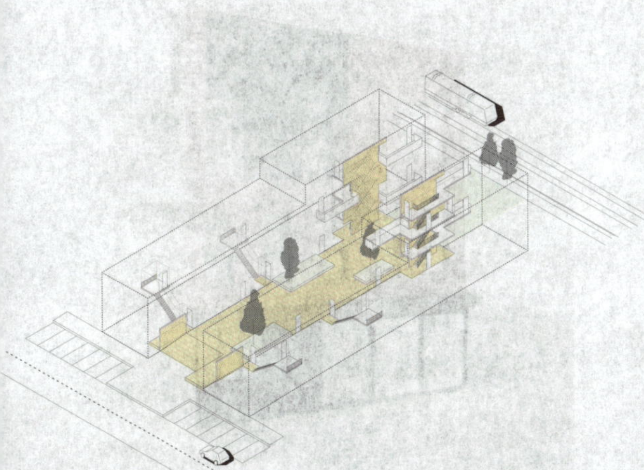

10

11

12

7. PIB, Single-family house, Beigem-Grimbergen   8. WWL, Collective housing, Leuven   9. XLB, Housing, Beveren
10. BCW, Refectory, Woumen   11. KPG, Single-family house, Ghent   12. WWL, Collective housing, Leuven

1

2

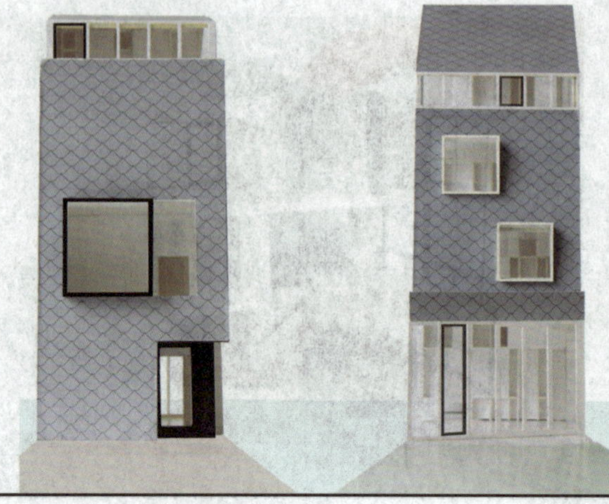

3

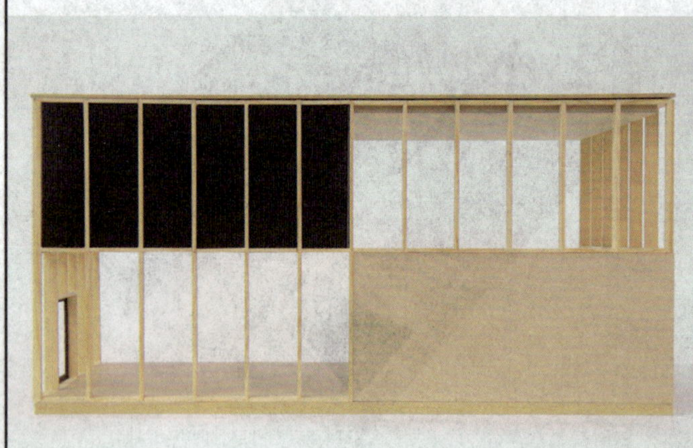

4

5

6

1. BBA, Primary school, Antwerp 2. KBA, Single-family house, Ghent 3. KAU, Gymnasium, Uccle
4. JHU, Two-family house, Uccle 5. WWL, Collective housing, Leuven 6. FAR, Single-family house, Rumbeke

7

8

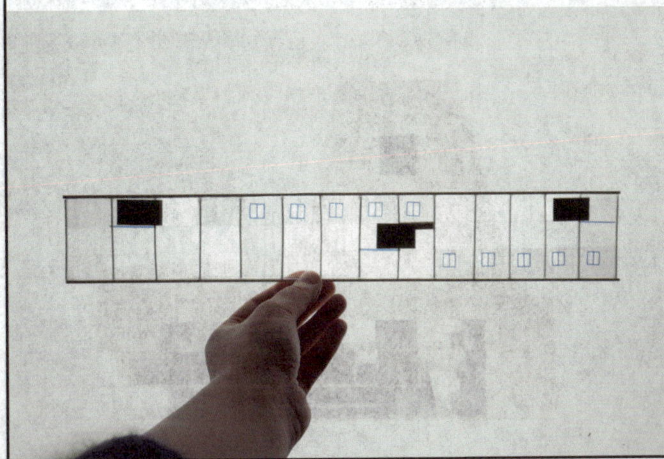

9

10

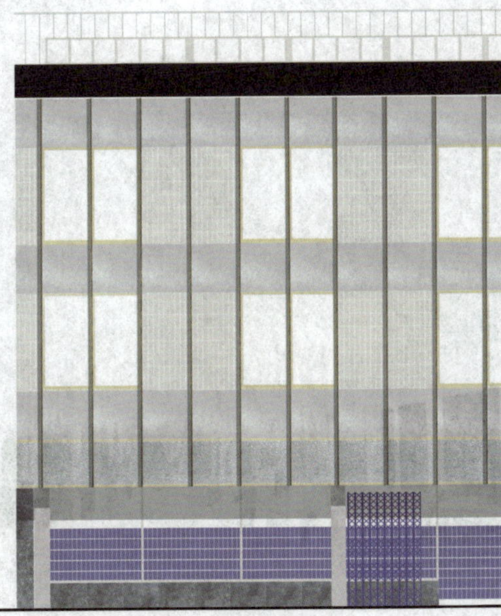

11

12

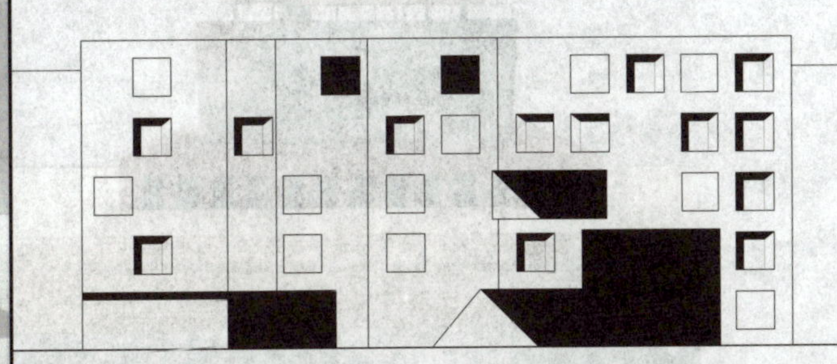

7. PZE, Multipurpose hall, Eeklo 8. AQA, Campus Aquafin, Aartselaar 9. WZK, Residential care centre, Kortrijk 10. BBA, Primary school, Antwerp 11. MDD, Collective housing, Deinze 12. WAL, Stacked houses, Ghent

1

2

3

4

5

6

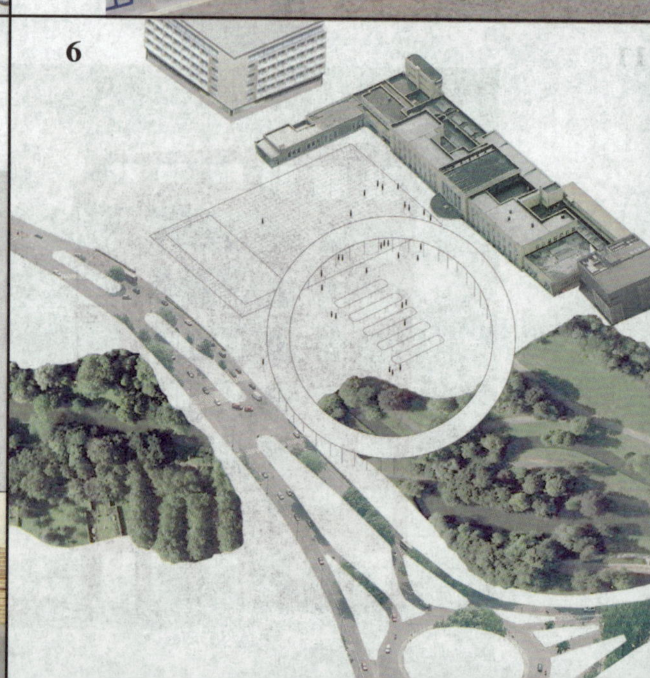

1. WWL, Collective housing, Leuven 2. DPL, Offices and pavilion, Leuven 3. MPZ, Master plan rehabilitation centre, Zandhoven
4. AQA, Campus Aquafin, Aartselaar 5. JDC, House for an artist 6. BLB, Bus station, Bruges

7

8

9

10

11

12

7. KOP, Office and warehouse, Puurs 8. GOD, Conversion concrete power station, Ghent 9. MTL, Housing and retail, Leuven 10. JGK, Youth hostel, Kortrijk 11. HTB, Passenger port, Brussels 12. CIX, Housing, Antwerp

1

2

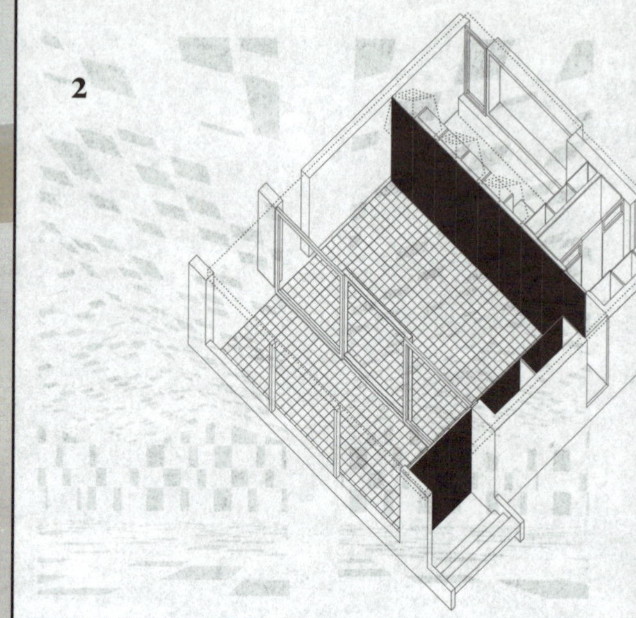

3

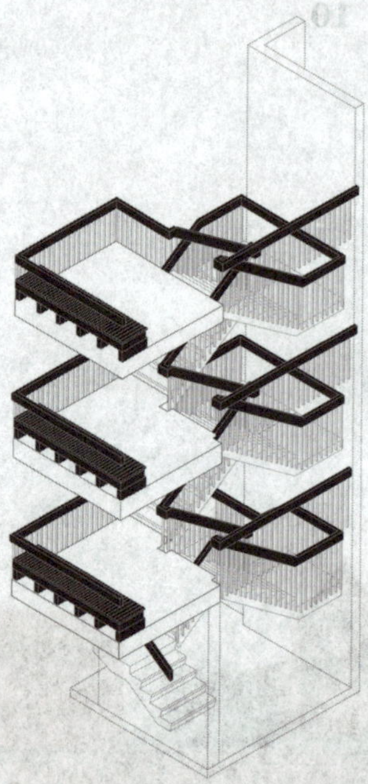

4

5

6

1. LWW, Canopy, Watou 2. JKB, Extension single-family house, Beersel 3. RLN, Rehabilitation centre, Ninove
4. BZB, Bozar scenography (Bruegel), Brussels 5. RLN, Rehabilitation centre, Ninove 6. OSB, Bus stop prototype, Brussels

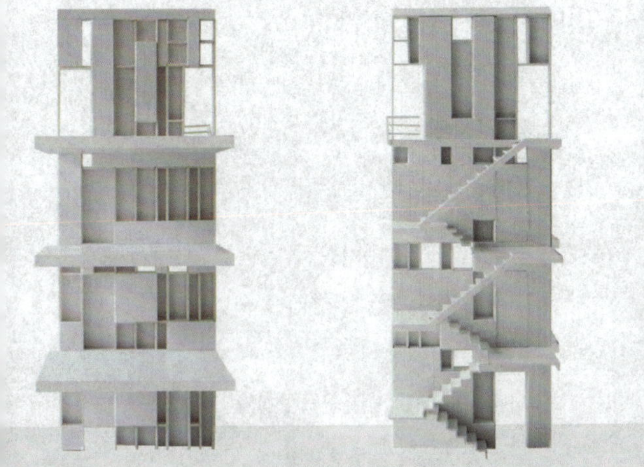

8

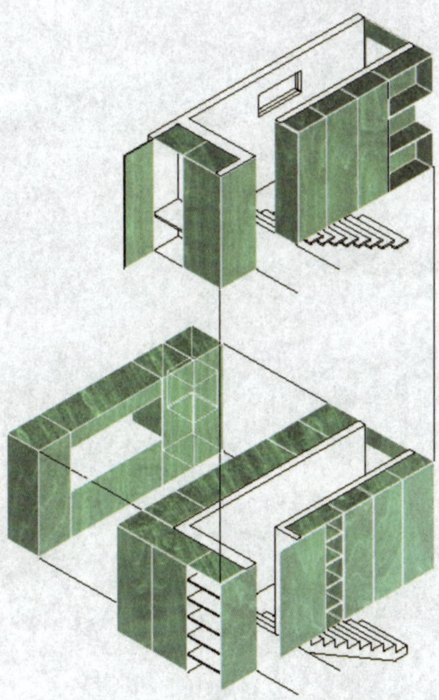

10

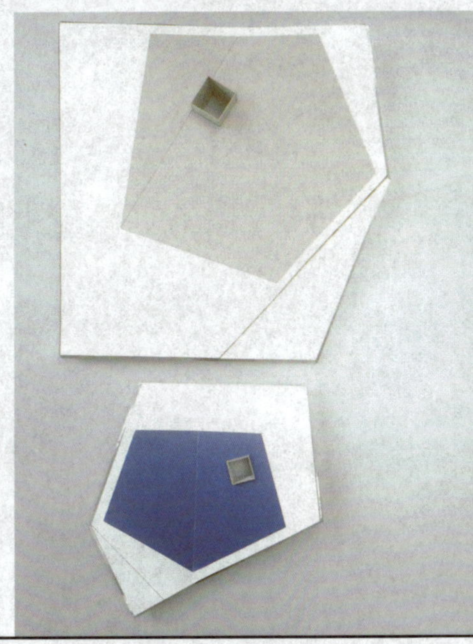

11

12

7. KPG, Single-family house, Ghent 8. DPL, Offices and pavilion, Leuven 9. OAV, Renovation single-family house, Tervuren
10. JGE, Community spaces, Brussels 11. BVD, Extension single-family house, Dilbeek
12. BVD, Extension single-family house, Dilbeek

7. KPG, Single-family house, Ghent 8. DPL, Offices and pavilion, Leuven 9. DAV, Renovation single-family house, Tervuren
10. JGE, Communal spaces, Brussels 11. HVD, Extension single-family house, Dilbeek
12. HVD, Extension single-family house, Dilbeek

Projects

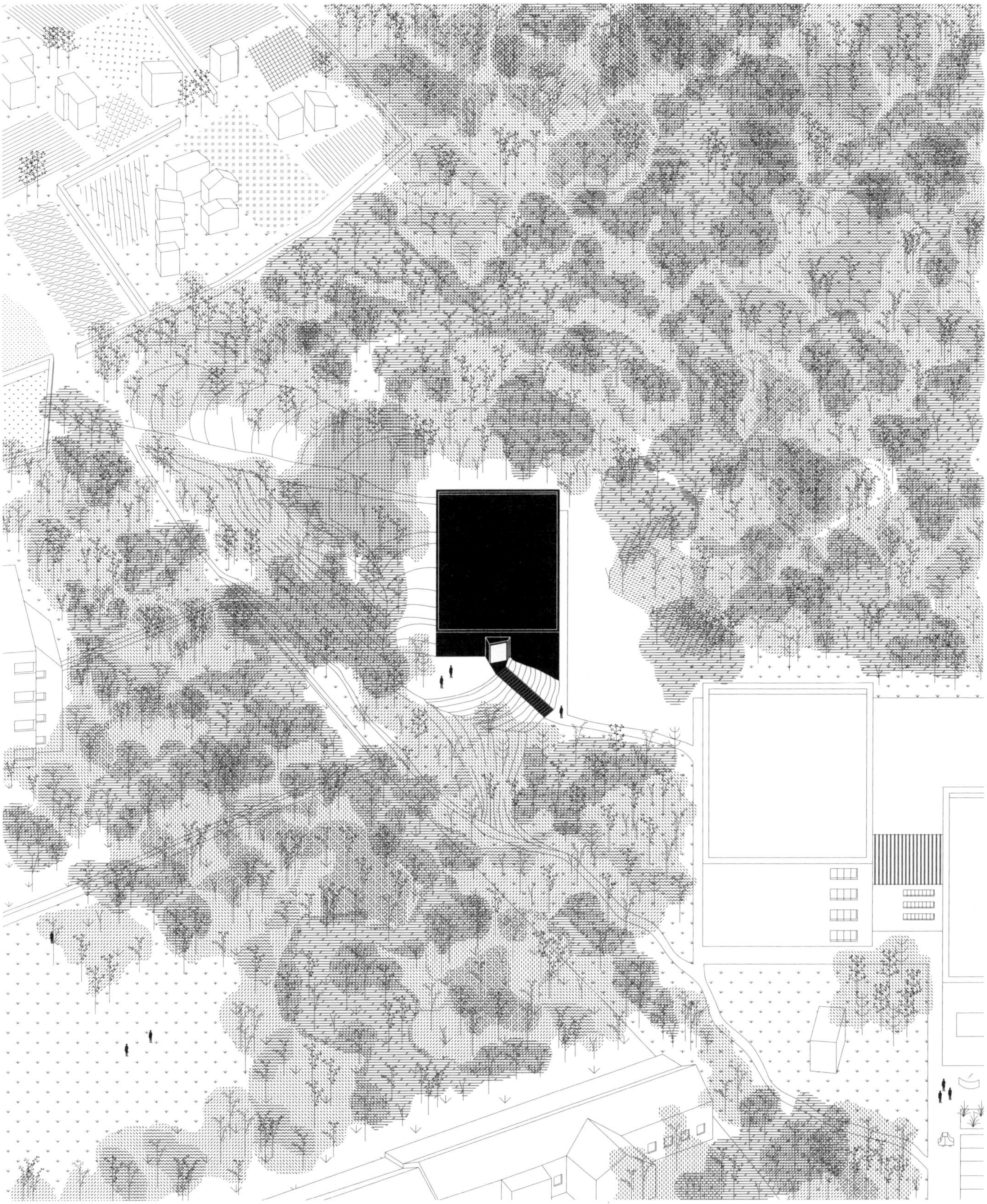

Uccle (Brussels)

This sports hall was commissioned by the *Athénée royal* of Uccle, a municipality in the south of Brussels. It is one of URA's best-known buildings. Its complex genesis bears witness to the idiosyncratic attitude of the architects. During the competition phase, they decided not to design the hall as an extension of the school building, as prescribed by the competition brief, but proposed a separate pavilion. This violation of the competition conditions initially earned them a second place but, because the winning competition fell through, their gymnasium was ultimately built.

URA's questioning attitude recurs in the design of this meticulously elaborated box. In order to embed the voluminous hall seamlessly in its surroundings, they half buried the construction in the sloping topography. Instead of drawing the usual black box, they engaged with the wooded environment through façade-wide window openings on three sides of the volume. With the roots and trunks of trees on one side, and canopies on the other, a perfect filter is created against the low sunlight.

The entrance is shaped by a sculptural concrete element which acts as both outdoor stair and entrance hall, and which, on the inside, forms a small stand and serves to organize the functional area with changing rooms and sanitary facilities.

The contextual location is extended in the lightness of the construction as a whole, whose steel structure disappears behind the woodwork. Thanks to a set of contrasts between materials – concrete and black corrugated aluminium plates outdoors; pine plywood, concrete blocks and tiling indoors – URA managed to create a surprisingly elegant building on a limited budget. [is]

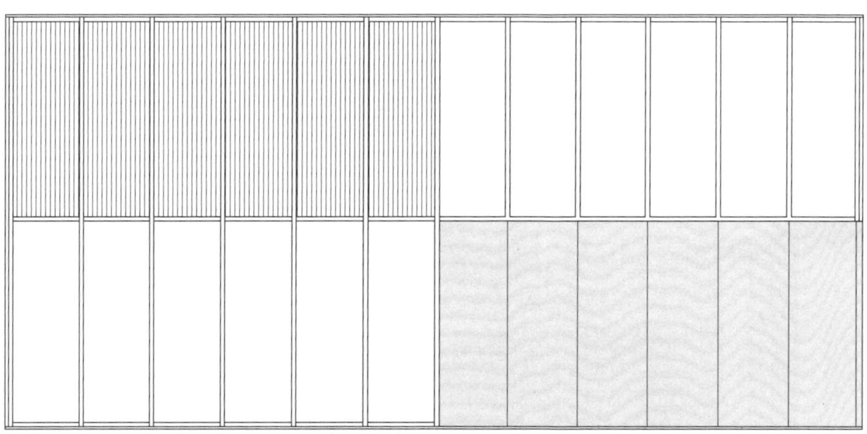

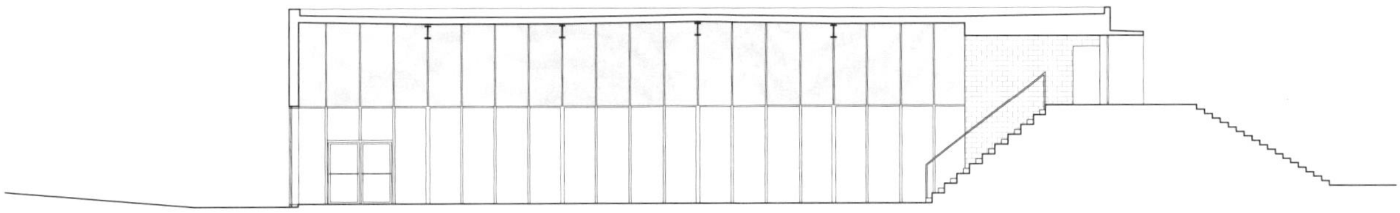

Section Aa

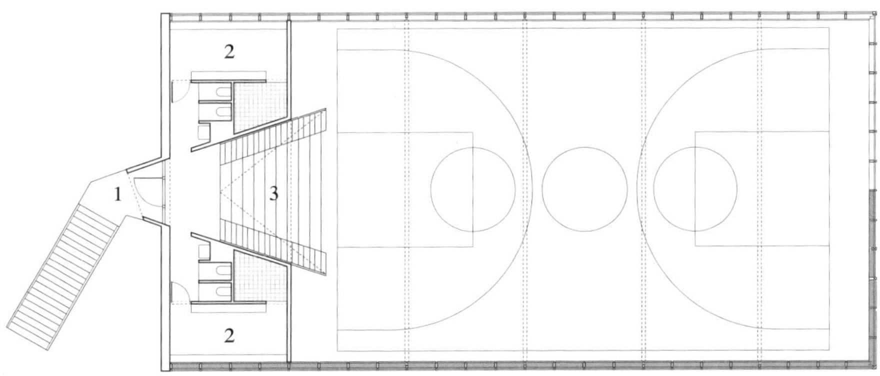

Floor 1

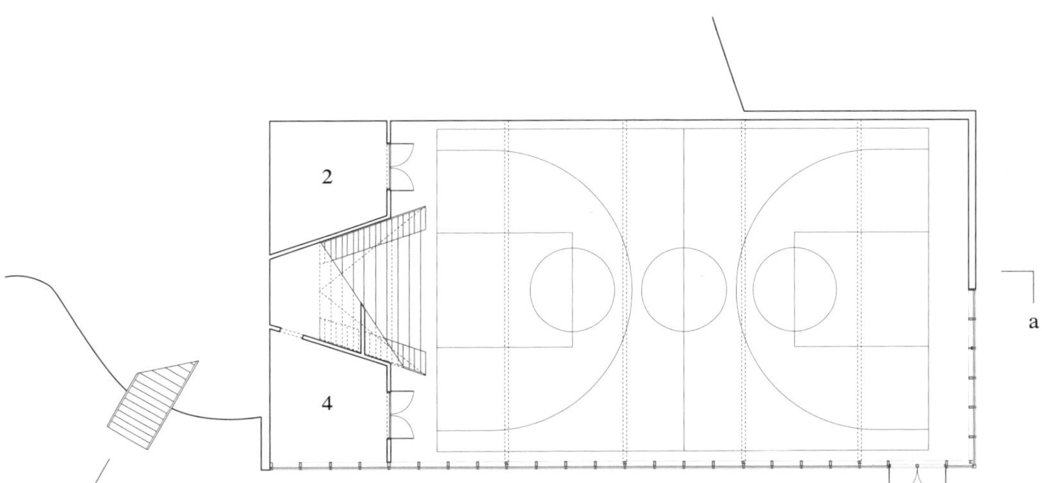

Floor 0

1 entrance
2 changing room
3 grandstand
4 storage

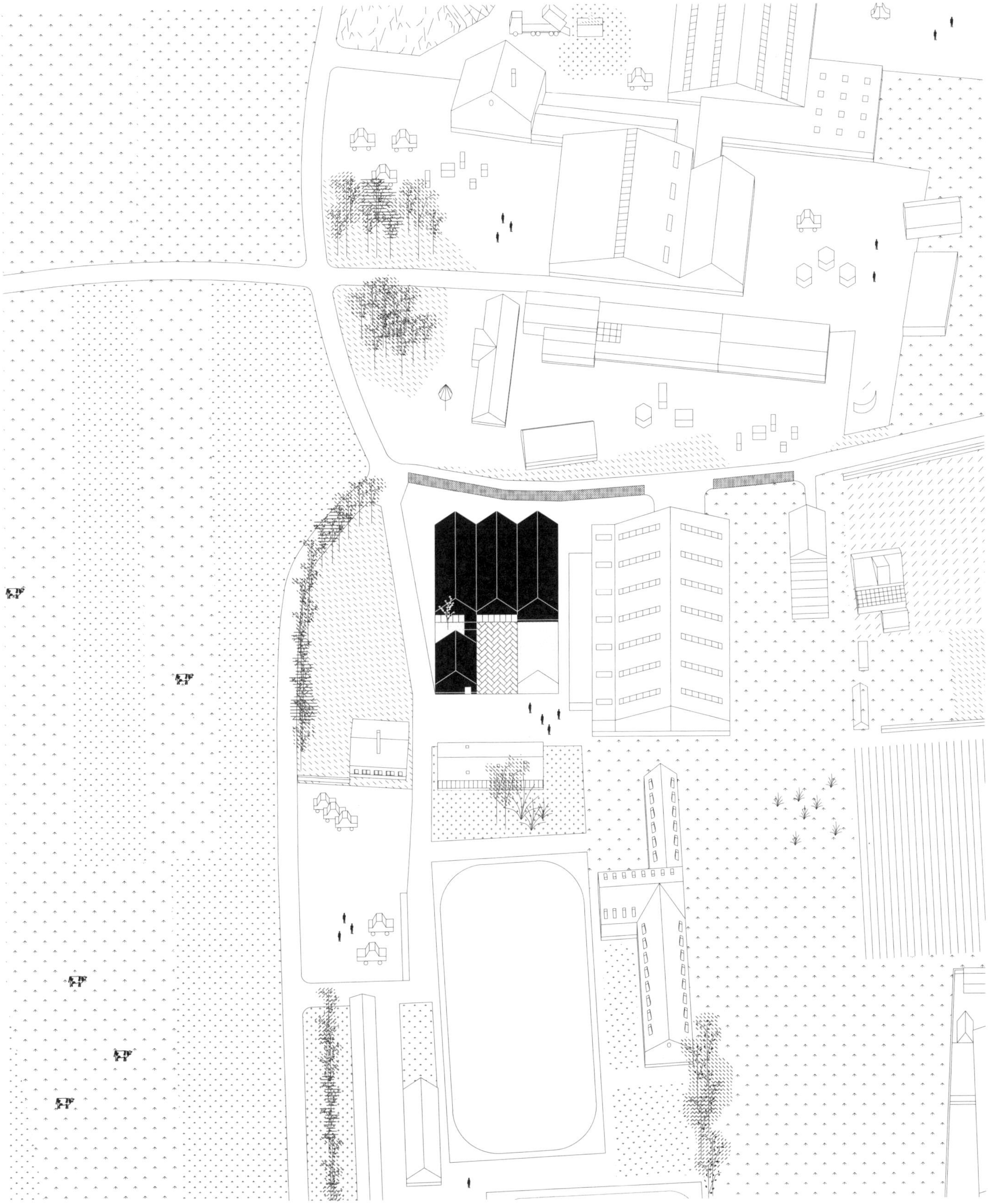

The equestrian sports centre of Sport Vlaanderen, the Flemish sports agency, in Woumen is located in an idyllic environment in the middle of the polders to the south of Diksmuide. The site comprises a range of sleeping facilities as well as stables and paddocks. An application was made via a DBFM procedure to add a multipurpose hall with an industrial kitchen as well as separate sanitary facilities. URA's winning competition design also included a separate volume with a classroom, which was ultimately not built: instead, an extension of the outdoor space was made possible.

In terms of typology, URA ensured the new buildings tied in with the existing constructions: whitewashed brick sheds with traditional saddle roofs and black-tarred bases. The result is two concrete volumes with rectangular window openings along the edge of the plot which, owing to the sophisticated detailing, come across as almost abstract apparitions. Because the concrete of the outer façade is also used in the fibre cement of the roof's corrugated iron, the different volumes take on a uniformally monolithic character.

The refectory and the kitchen are housed in the trident that is connected, via a fine steel awning, to the smaller volume housing the sanitary facilitaties. This is where the children enter: there is room for them to remove their boots and to make their way to the refectory in their socks under the awning. The square window frame at seat height in the sanitary facilities is repeated four times in the dining area: a window onto the surroundings that the children can literally occupy. The black base of the volumes that also encircles the sandpit outside is echoed indoors in the brown wainscoting in which the heating elements are embedded and that becomes a bench in front of the low window openings. [is]

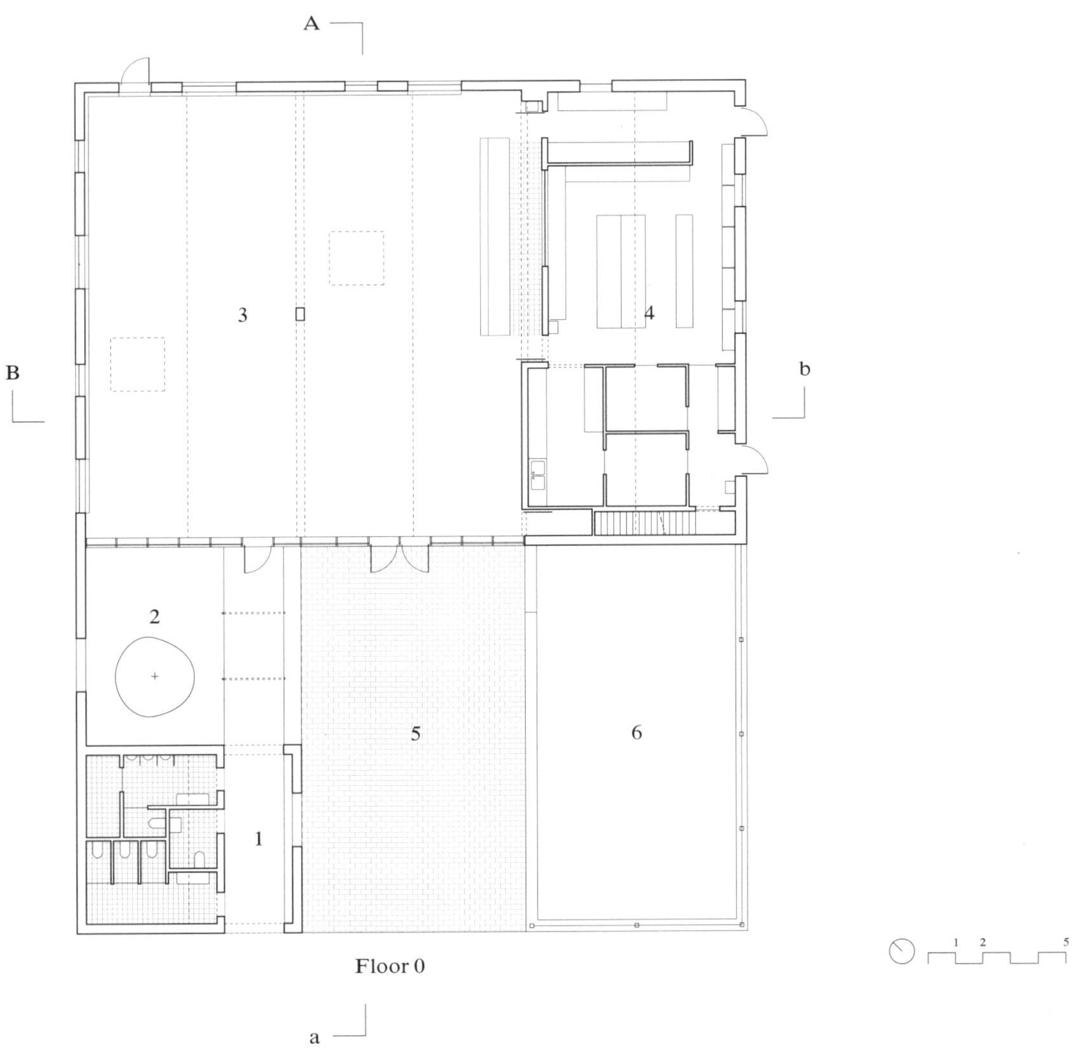

Floor 0

1 gallery
2 patio
3 refectory
4 kitchen
5 courtyard
6 sandpit

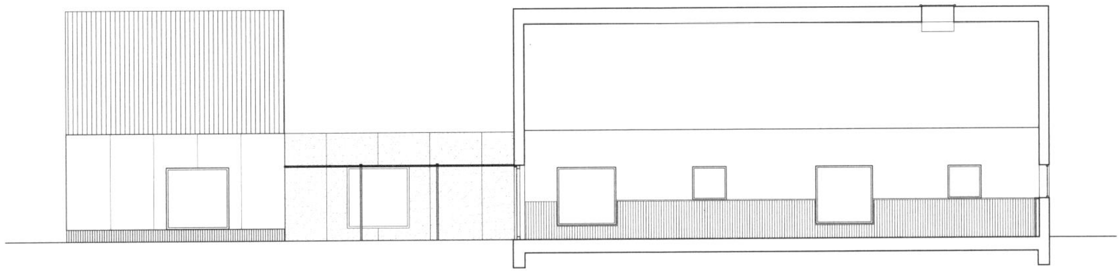

Section Aa

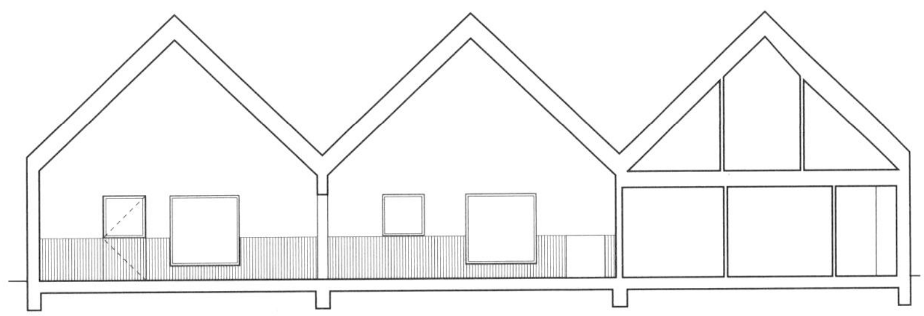

Section Bb

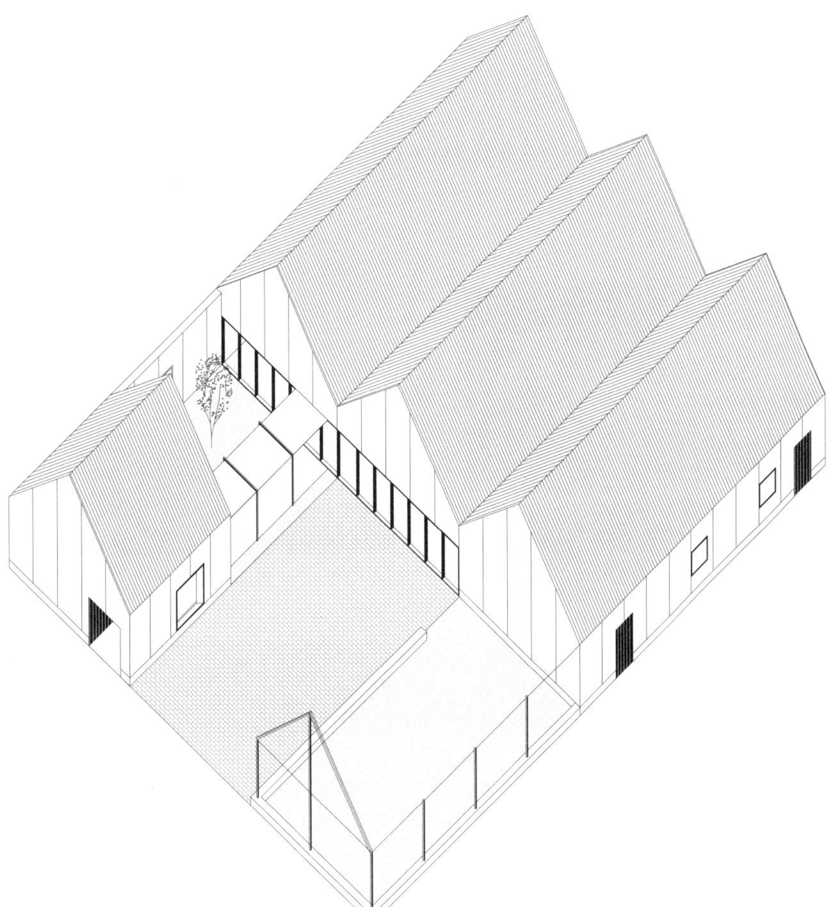

URA emptied out the school site enclosed between Rue Mathieu Desmaré and Avenue du Parc Royal. They freed up the dense inner area to make room for a large, rectangular playground. This outdoor space defines the project. It is a clear geometric delimitation, the condition around which construction happens. Literally. The volume of the kindergarten, on one side, and the primary school, on the other, have been pushed to the plot's edges.

The school gate has been kept on Rue Desmaré, a safer thoroughfare that branches off Avenue du Parc. From the street you have a view through to the playground, where a precisely planted tree serves as an eye-catcher. You enter the school through a funnel-shaped access between the administrative house with secretariat and the new main building of the primary school (years three to six). The ground floor is home to a sunken refectory, the top floor to a double-height gymnasium that functions as a lantern in the area. A telescopic window offers views onto the steeple of Laeken.

The kindergarten and the first and second years are housed in the converted nineteenth-century town house on Avenue du Parc. The architects decided to put the youngest children here on account of its homely character. The existing front façade has been preserved, with two classes behind it on each level. A second glass façade duplicates the rear façade; the built-on vertical winter garden accommodates a monumental open staircase. [ed]

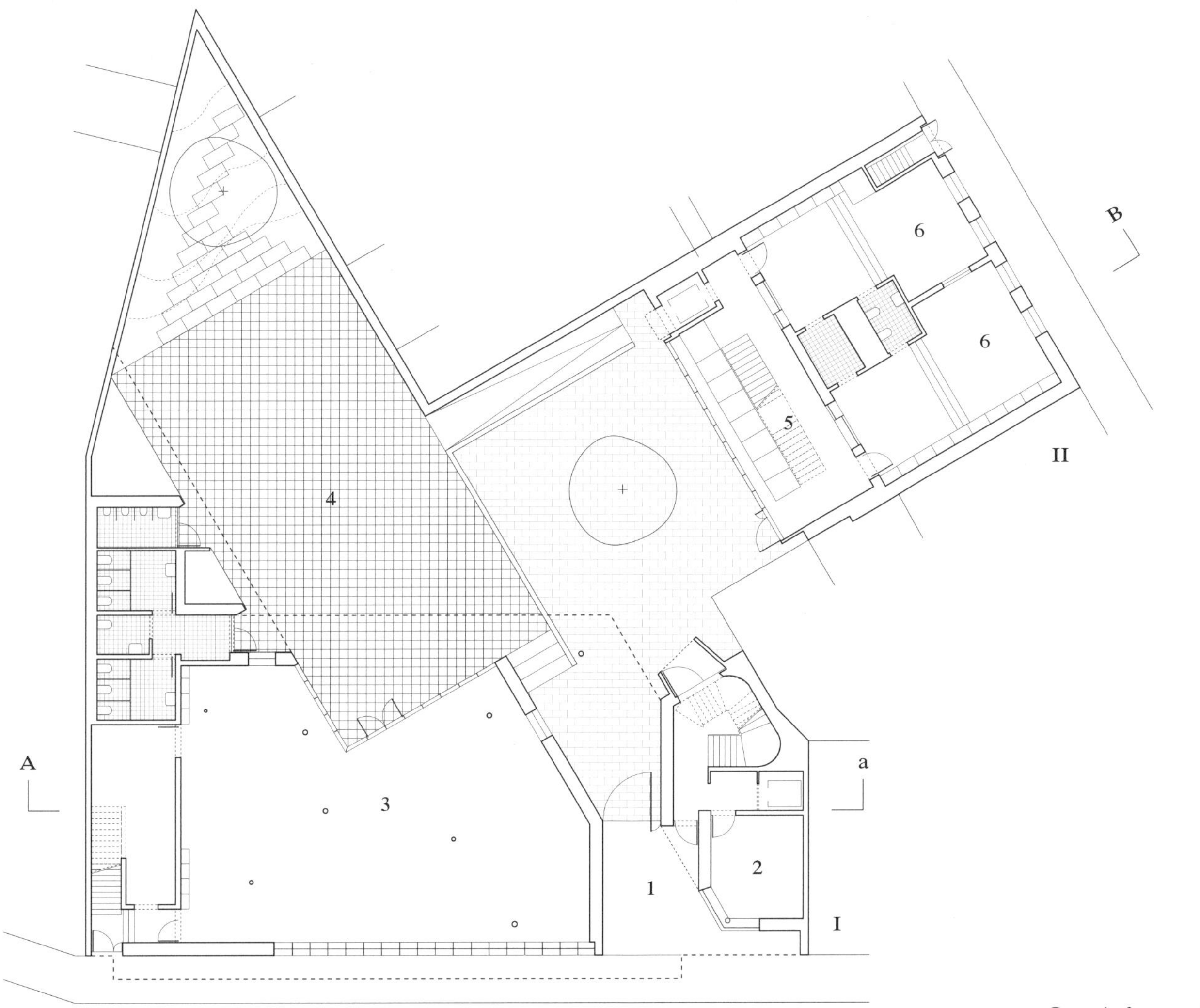

Floor 0

I Primary school
II Kindergarten

1 entrance
2 office
3 refectory
4 playground
5 glasshouse
6 classroom

Section Aa

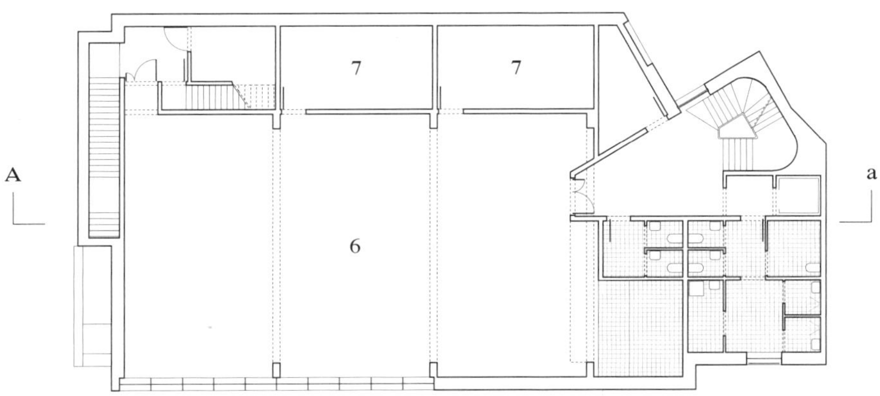

Floor 2

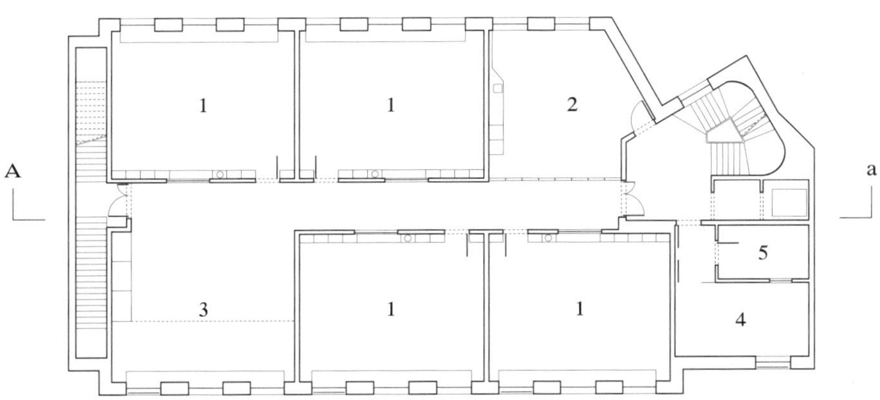

Floor 1

1 classroom
2 teacher's room
3 open classroom
4 director
5 first aid
6 sports hall
7 changing room

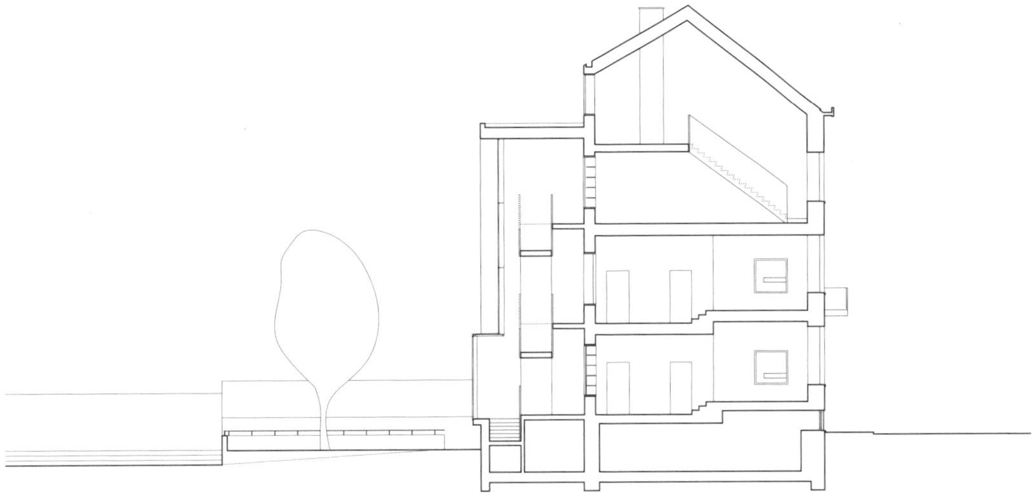

Section Bb

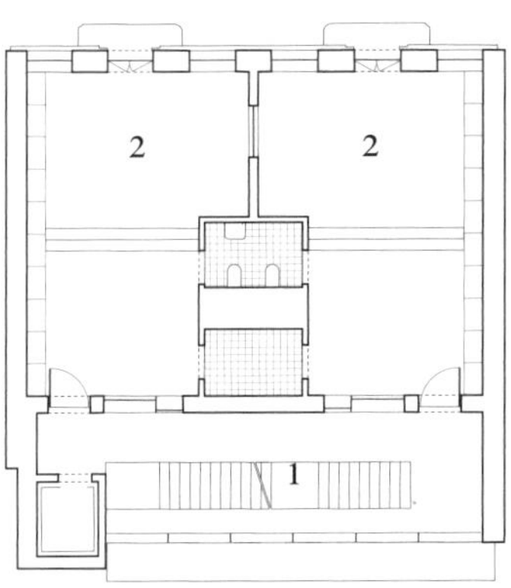

Floor 1

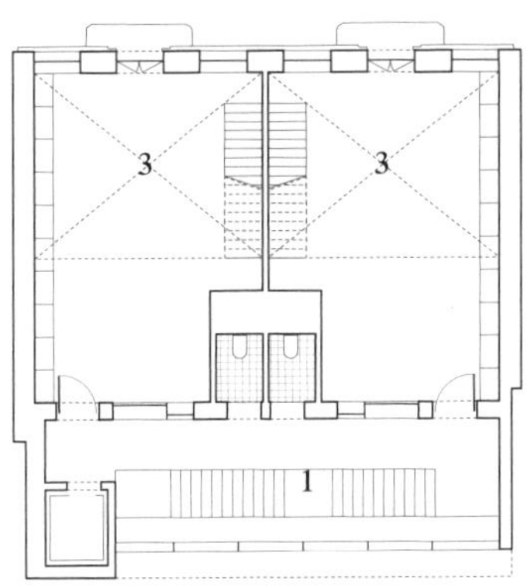

Floor 2

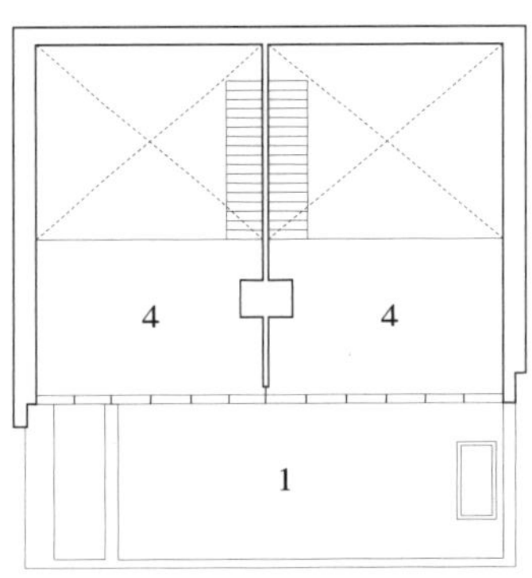

Floor 3

1 glass house
2 stage class
3 duplex class
4 duplex level

The project in Leuven provides offices for 80 employees and a meeting space for parents and children in 'Foster care Flemish Brabant and Brussels', an organization that assists children in search of a foster family.

Bounded by a thick retaining wall separating it from the road, the site benefits from a privileged, quiet location surrounded by vegetation, a genuine little island in the heart of the woods. In the middle of this enormous garden is a villa, the former house of the rector of Leuven University that was donated to the organization 'Pleegzorg Vlaanderen' (Foster care Flanders). Renovating the house seemed to be the most natural thing to do with regard to the home for children. However, as the project developed and grew more precise, it proved impossible to adapt the different needs to the existing structure and to bring it up to standard in terms of insulation. It was then decided to demolish it. However, the eminent white-brick façade with blue shutters inspired the institution's new administrative centre.

Three new constructions emerged: a large office building housing the institution's administrative headquarters, a pavilion with a multipurpose room (the house for the children and families), and a workshop around a red-brick courtyard. Each building has its own specific typology, as remarkable in terms of the façade as it is indoors, as required by the different programmes. In the past, the house featured exterior vertical circulation, which was separate from the building. It is now in the main building: a staircase surrounded by glass bricks providing employees with a moment's breath. The pavilion has generously glazed façades offering spaces open to the outside and connecting with the garden, covered by a light gable roof reminiscent of the typical ones found in houses in the region.

One of the main challenges was probably to imagine this new ensemble, even as the project was based on the reinterpretation of a building that had disappeared. The architects here took a stand with regard to their role, working as interpreters of a past and present physical context, with the measured apprehension of gestures and cohabitations. [fcn]

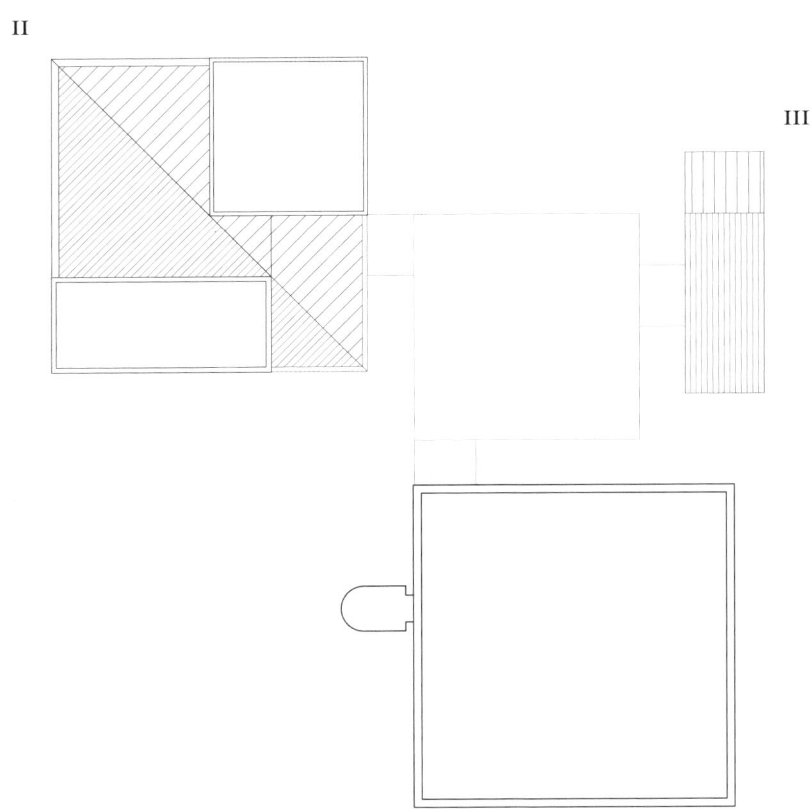

I Headquarter offices
II Pavilion
III Atelier

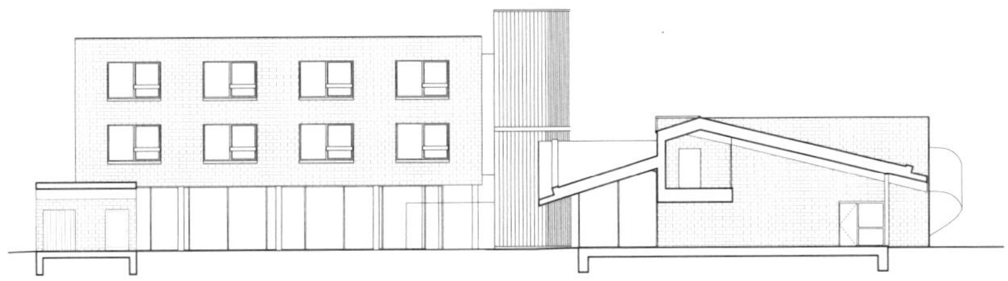

Section Aa

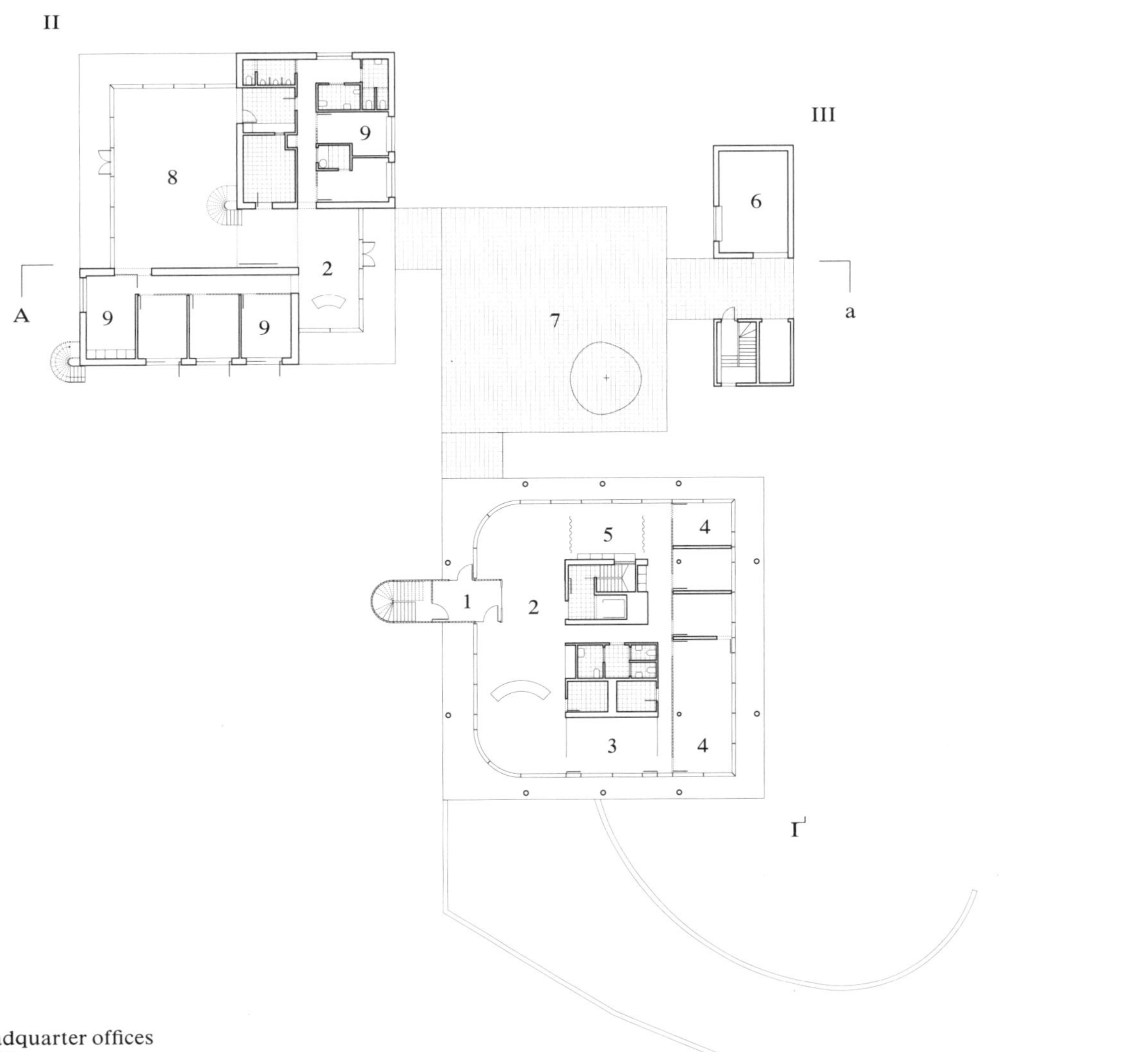

Floor 0

I Headquarter offices
II Pavilion
III Atelier

1 entrance
2 lobby
3 office
4 meeting room
5 library
6 workshop
7 square
8 foyer
9 family room

Section Bb

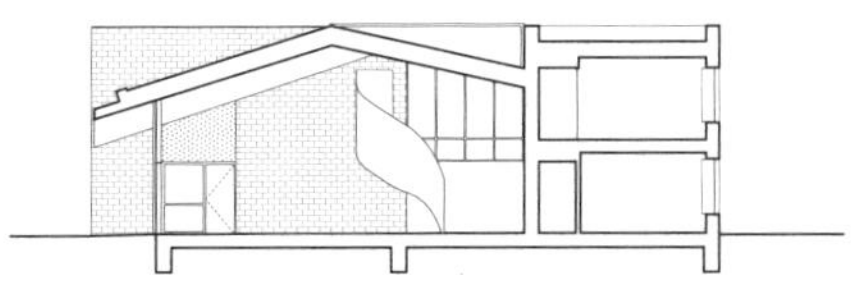

Section Cc

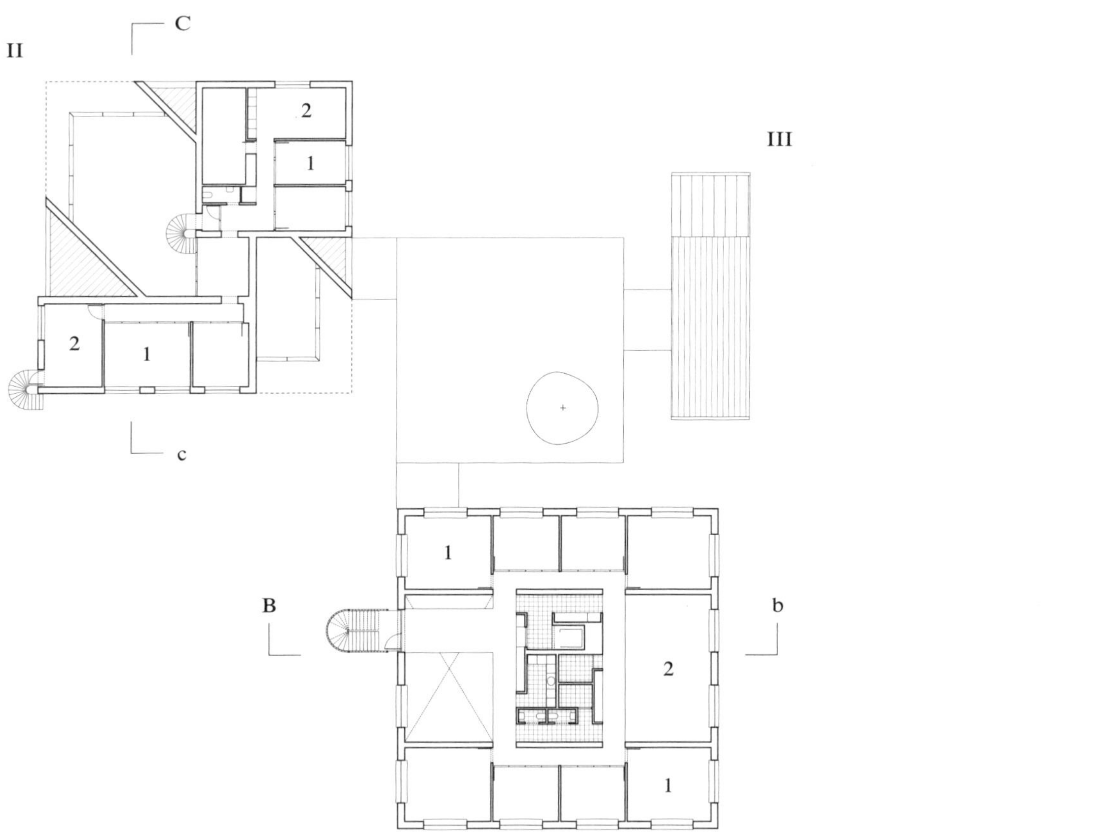

Floor 1

I Headquarter offices
II Pavilion
III Atelier

1 office
2 coworking

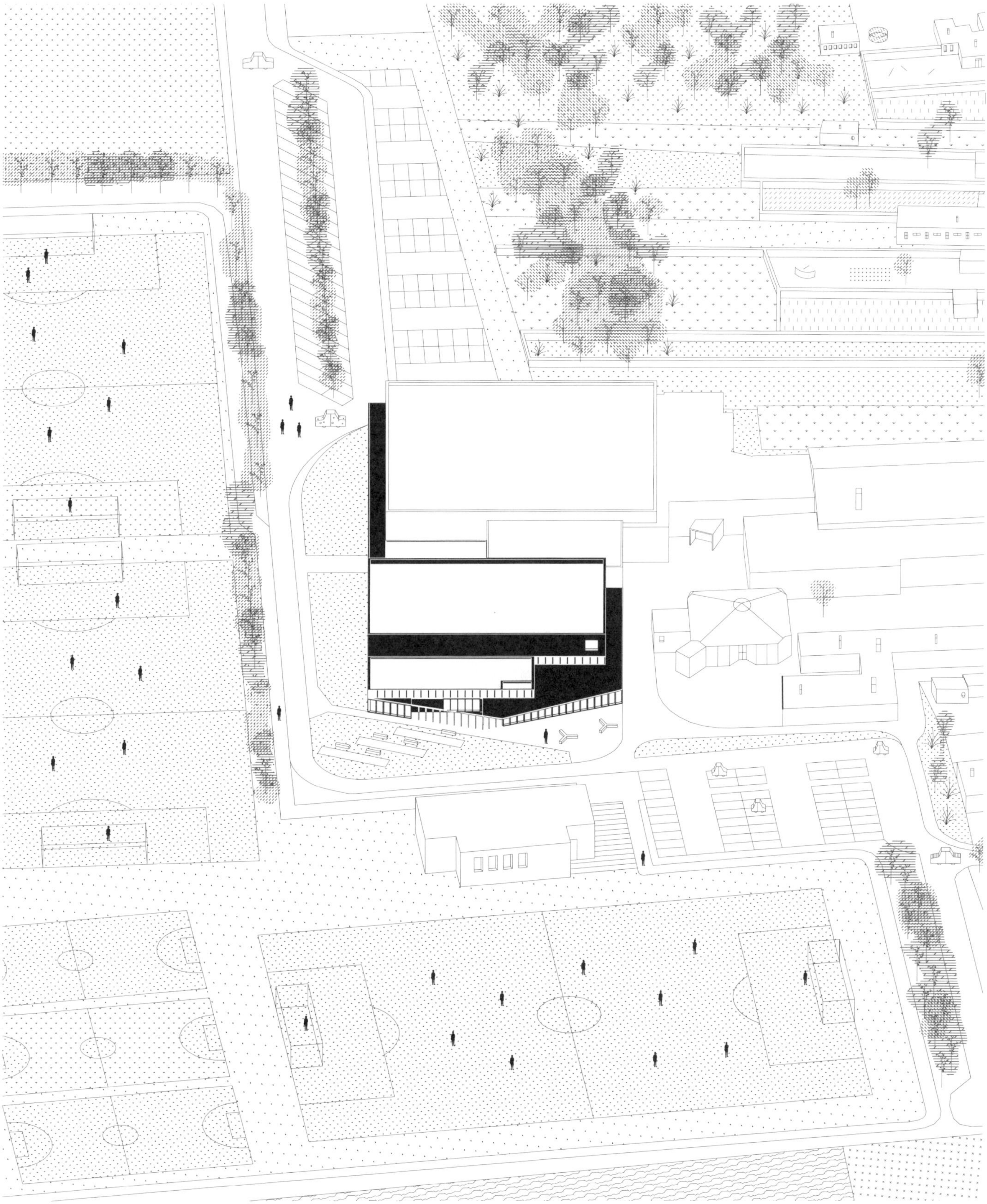

Nazareth is a municipality located in East Flanders, near Ghent. It is one of those historical villages that have become small residential towns, surrounded by agricultural fields and close to a motorway network. A suburban environment that is, after all, rather ordinary, but no less stimulating in terms of programme and architectural layout.

The need for the municipality to create a new gymnasium and a youth centre near an existing sports hall – of questionable typology, given its massiveness, a gigantic, windowless concrete block – and close to other outdoor sports facilities (football fields), car parks and other fields constituted a real challenge in terms of integration.

Two new buildings were erected on the site of the sports hall. A refined aluminium structure extends around the complex, creating a covered walkway that connects the buildings to the outside, giving the site a new legibility in rela-tion to its surroundings. The dimensions of this structure find their source in the hall's existing infrastructure, adapted to the human scale and their uses; the same applies to that of the new gymnasium, which is moreover aligned on the height of the sports hall.

Thanks to two openings located on the south façade, the hall benefits from entrances and exits connected to the covered circulation space. Several openings have been made on the east façade so that the new gymnasium can share its changing rooms with the hall. This gesture also made it possible to integrate the hall building into the overall plan. Generally speaking, each of the buildings offers one or more forms of direct interaction with the neighbouring building. Moreover, although covered with corrugated iron, the gymnasium reproduces the impression of a closed block from the outside, like its imposing neighbour.

The youth centre, which is quite glazed, has rooms that are bathed in natural light as well as generous outdoor spaces. The youth centre and the new gymnasium form a compact entity, built up against the hall, thus freeing up a lot of space outside, which is necessary for the new configuration of the area.

Three different building materials and scales stand out and give the whole a layered and sequenced character, revealing the site's new anchorage and identity. The redefinition of overall and domestic scales in relation to the environment was also what was missing in the latter: the infrastructure now forms a remarkable ensemble, at once integrated and multiple, and turned towards the rural landscape. [fcn]

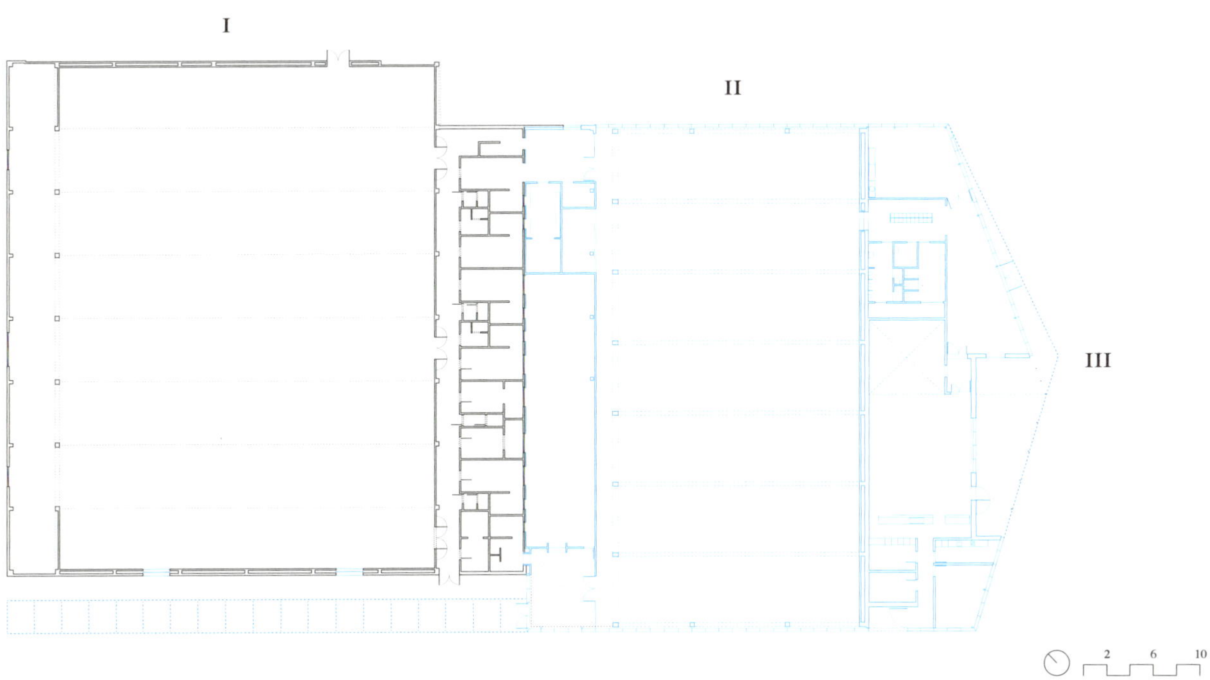

I Existing sports hall
II New gymnasium
II Youth centre

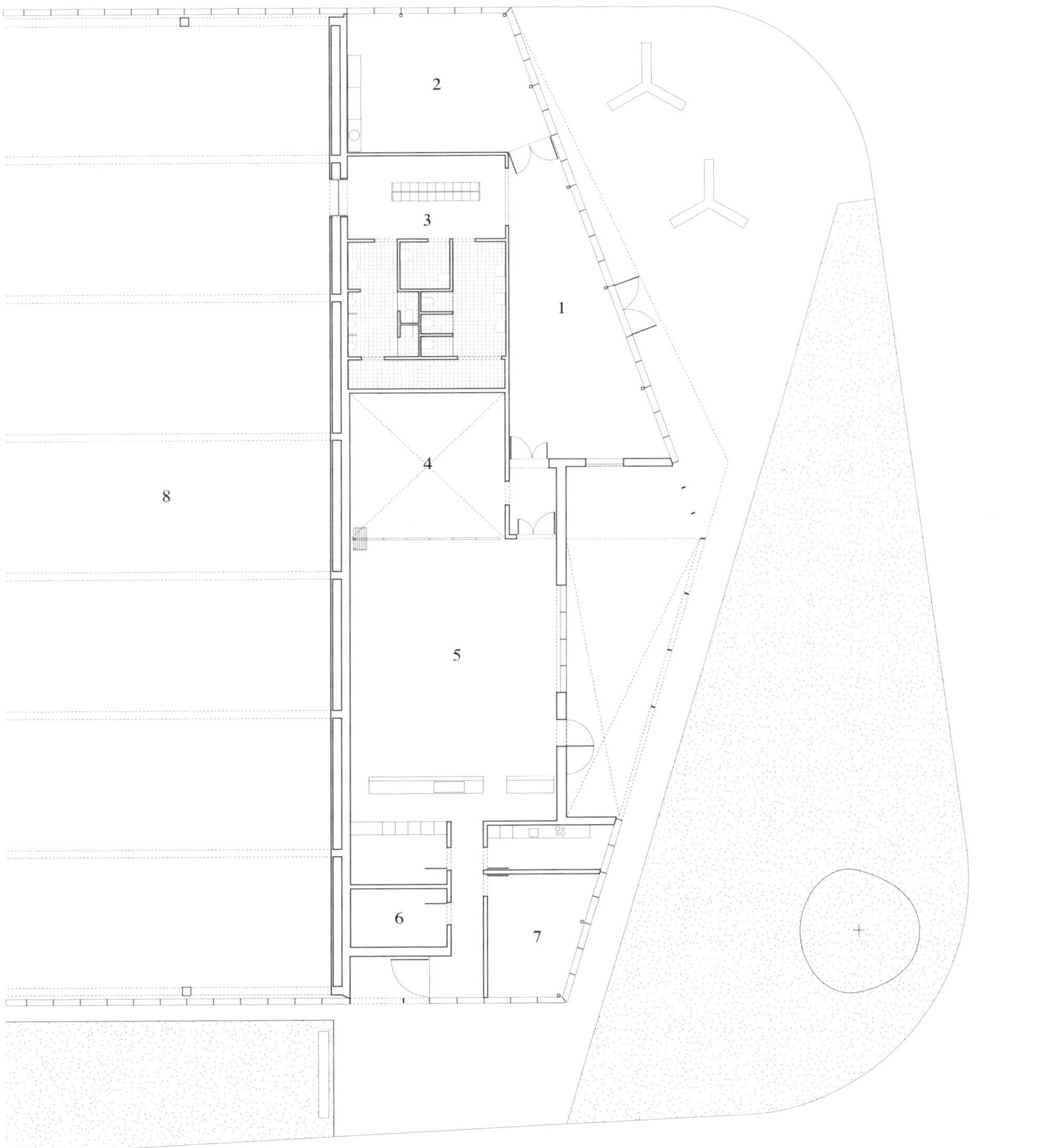

Floor 0

1 lobby
2 workshop
3 cloakroom
4 rehearsal room
5 youth centre
6 storage
7 meeting room
8 gymnasium

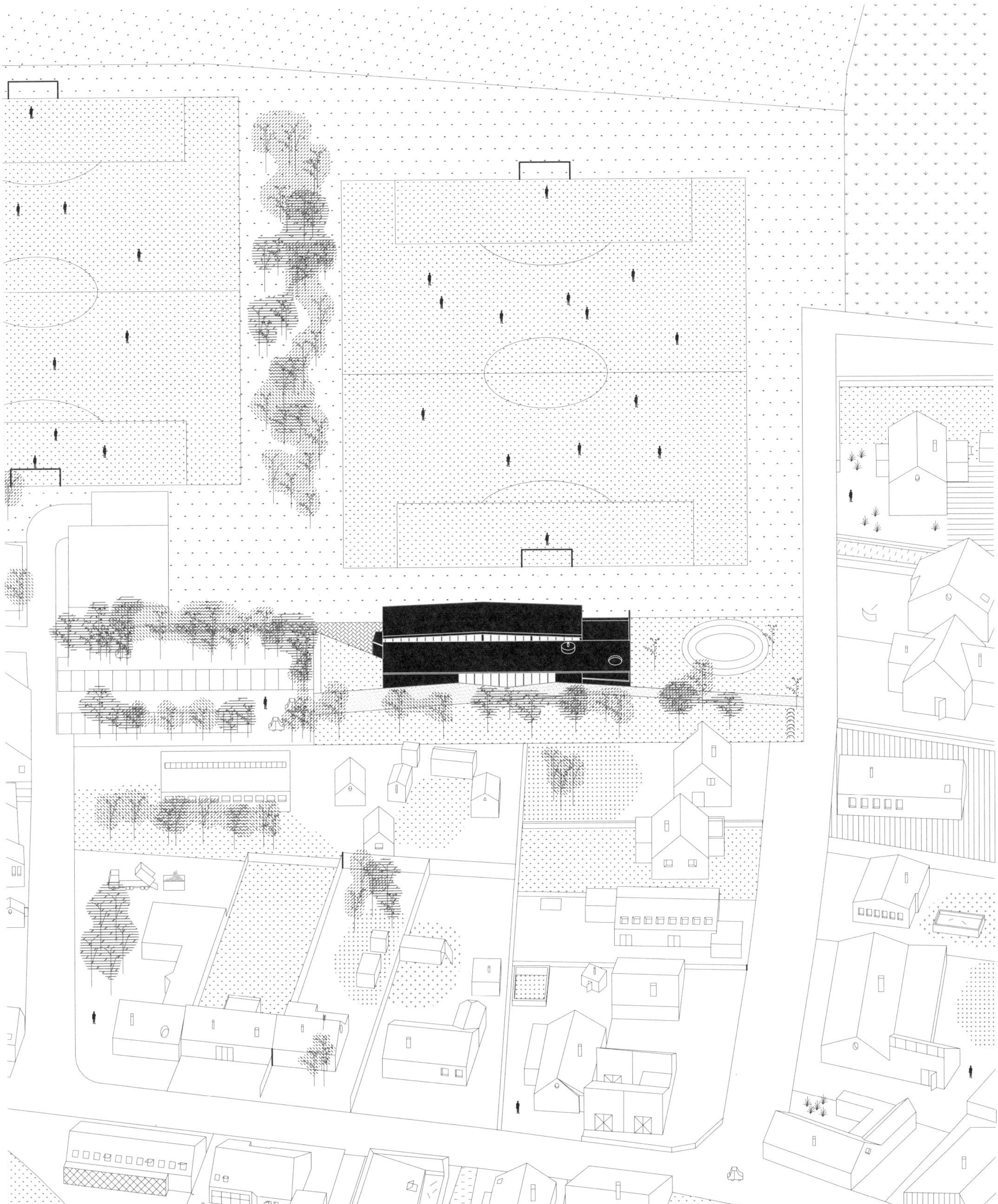

Erected on the edge of an allotment with a crease in the landscape, this small community infrastructure offers a panoramic view of football pitches and agricultural lands. In their winning competition design, URA imagined the little building as a shed that, like many industrial buildings in the environment, was made out of corrugated iron. And yet the construction transcends a purely functional logic – on the one hand, because it lets in natural light via a long horizontal skylight on the ridge, and on the other hand, because a complex strategy unfolds inside with a succession of perforated walls that organize and set out the programme, but also play a structural role. Designed as outdoor façades, these concrete transverse walls, with their ochre-coloured sliding doors, make it possible for the multi-purpose space to be annexed by either the football canteen or by one of the two rooms of the after-school childcare. In the last, partly covered bay, an outdoor space is created that is integrated naturally and elegantly within the borders of the built volume and was given a balustrade in the same ochre colour. The playful round hole in the roof refers to the cylindrical volume that accommodates the technical facilities and is located a bit further on top of the volume. Thanks to a zigzagging façade at the front and the slightly inclined roof at the rear, the architects have grafted the building into its context. [is]

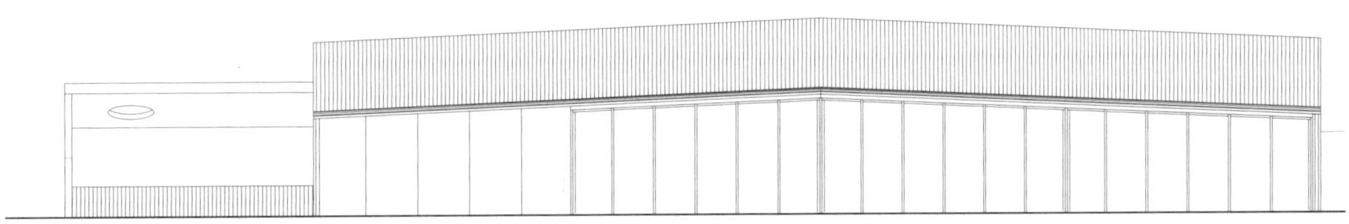

North elevation

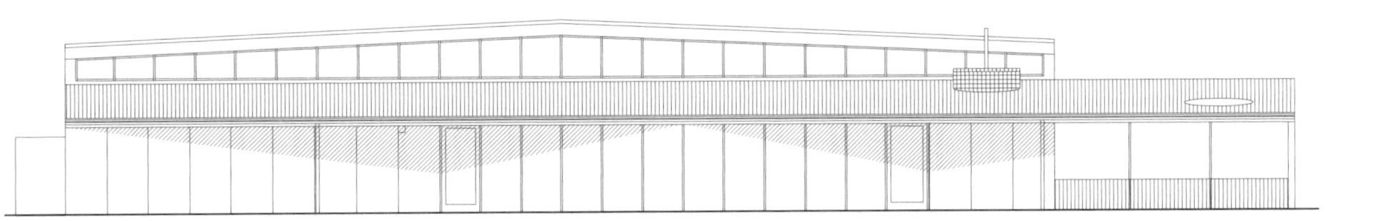

South elevation

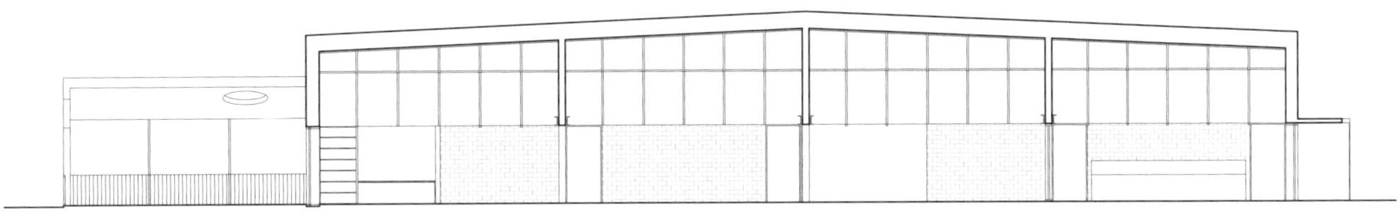

Section Aa

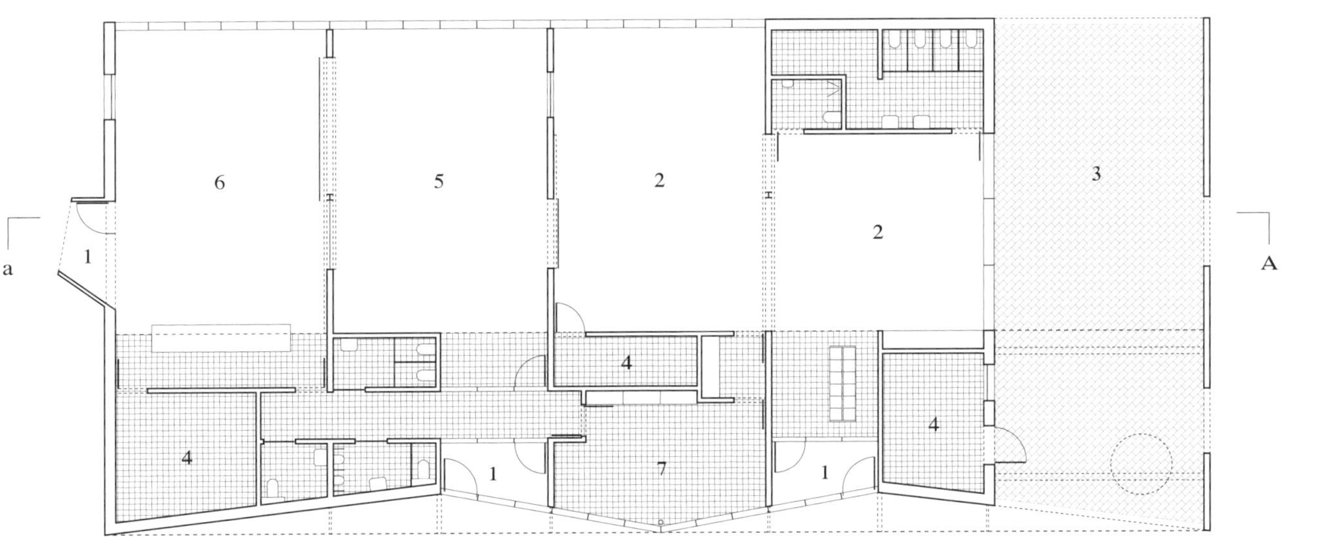

Floor 0

1 entrance
2 after-school childcare
3 playground
4 storage
5 hall
6 football canteen
7 meeting room

Cross sections

Gasthof De Eendracht

2018 LWW Canopy

A small shelter for the bus to Ypres on Watouplein: URA's proposal for this modest assignment was retained after a competition organized by WinVorm (Province of West Flanders).

The context of the Watou Arts Festival – in which poetry, visual art and the agricultural environment are woven together annually – and the historical significance of the square and church meant that a banal little bus shelter almost had to be elevated to the level of art.

The seemingly operational assignment soon proved to be a pretext to rethink the entire square. This involved controlling the traffic flow, arranging parking spaces, planting trees, and moving and restoring artworks.

The square was hardly touched on. A pot of white paint was all that was needed to control the traffic flow and change the parking spaces, while trees were limited to the west side. The intervention planned on the south side was granted more space and given greater visibility and significance.

The unhurried time span and the modesty of the project ensured that the designers could work out the assignment down to the smallest details. It became an extensive concrete canopy with a few wooden, glass and steel elements.

The slightly sloping butterfly roof rests on two trapeze-shaped pillars into which wooden furniture has been integrated. There is a sheltered bench for the bus on one side, and an open picnic area on the other. Thanks to the fold in the roof, the rainwater runs to the middle before disappearing into the underground sewer system via four steel pillars. These slim posts serve to ensure not only the span and evacuation, but also a visual transition between two functional zones.

Watou has already appropriated this concrete sculpture by URA. The bicycle parking designed by the architects has been extended with extra bike racks and more functional street furniture. '*La vie a raison*', as Le Corbusier knew, and as the architecture acknowledges here too. [fc]

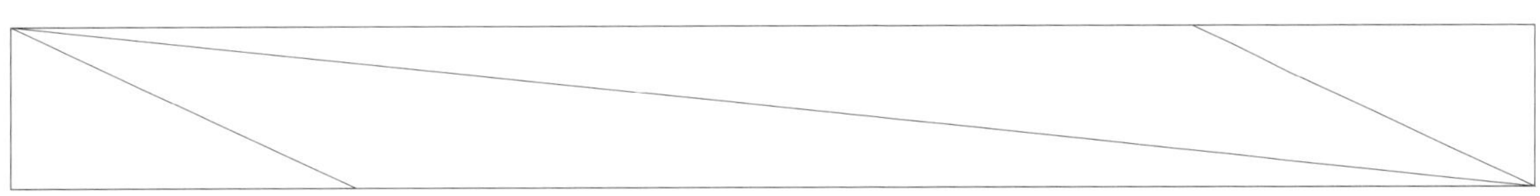

Roof plan

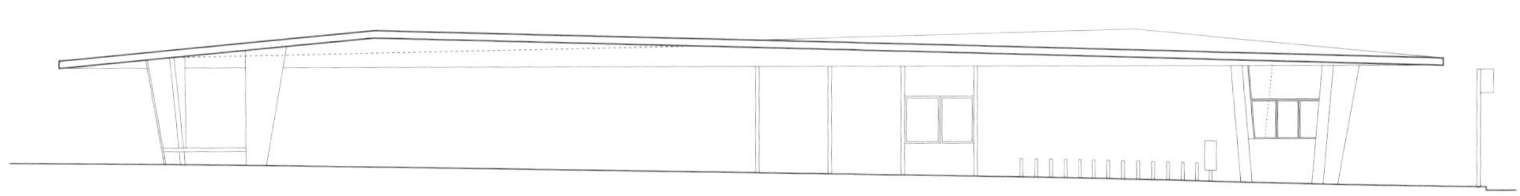

South elevation

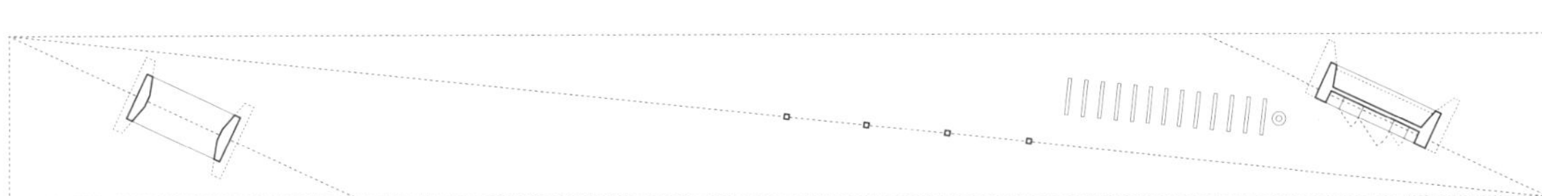

Floor 0

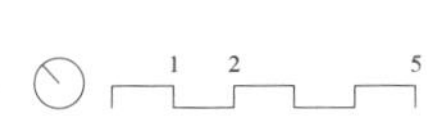

asthof De Eendrac

Gasthof De Eendracht
Kapittel

Elevation

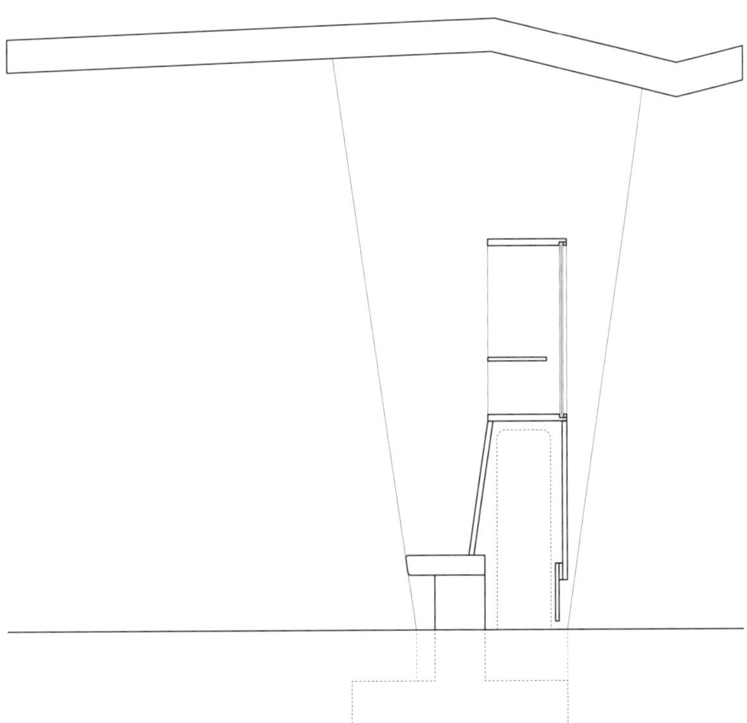

Section

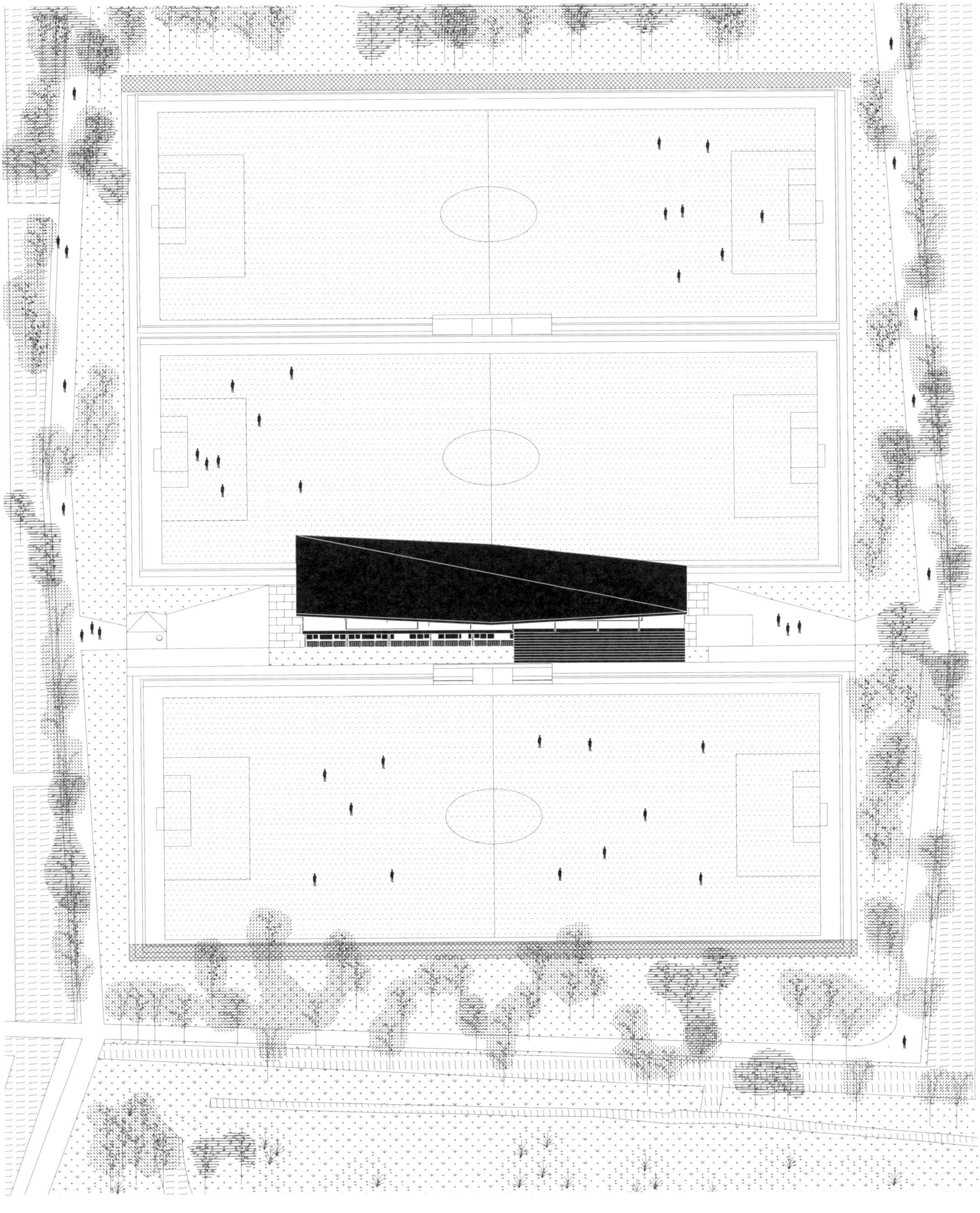

In 2015 URA designed the stadium building for a new sports park in Puurs, whose master plan was drawn up by BUUR. It is only after the definitive fusion of the municipalities of Puurs and Sint-Amands in 2018 that the municipal authorities returned to the plans. The project will be put out to tender in 2020.

The stadium is reachable via both a northern and southern access road, and has neither a specific front nor rear. The transverse shortcut in the middle of the building lies exactly in the axis of the middle line of the adjacent football pitches. The shower-equipped changing rooms are organized on the ground floor around a central core with sanitary and technical rooms. The first floor is home to a canteen which, because of the asymmetrically placed core, is divided into a large and small room. The main stand, which faces the main pitch, is accessible from the adjacent outdoor gallery and terraces. The stand on the northern side lies diagonally opposite the actual main entrance in the south; the circulation changes with the side and thus makes a circuit around the all-round building.

Everything has been collected under one oversize roof whose ridge runs diagonally across the two surfaces. The technical floor under the roof makes it possible to highlight the peak even more. This ensures that the building can strike a pose with regard to the artificial landscape of bald grass pitches. The tips of the roof are raised in a single movement, like a folded piece of paper. This enables the architects to create views from the terraces on both of the building's end sides. The roof is supported by massive wooden trusses: the porticos are tangibly present in the open space of the canteen.

The building is finished with sober materials: concrete blocks, prefab columns, glass, aluminium window frames, and galvanized sheets of corrugated metal for the parapet and the roof. The corridor along the changing rooms is an outdoor gallery: each door gives onto the outside and has a 'house number', an outdoor light and a bench to watch the training or to wait for the players. [ed]

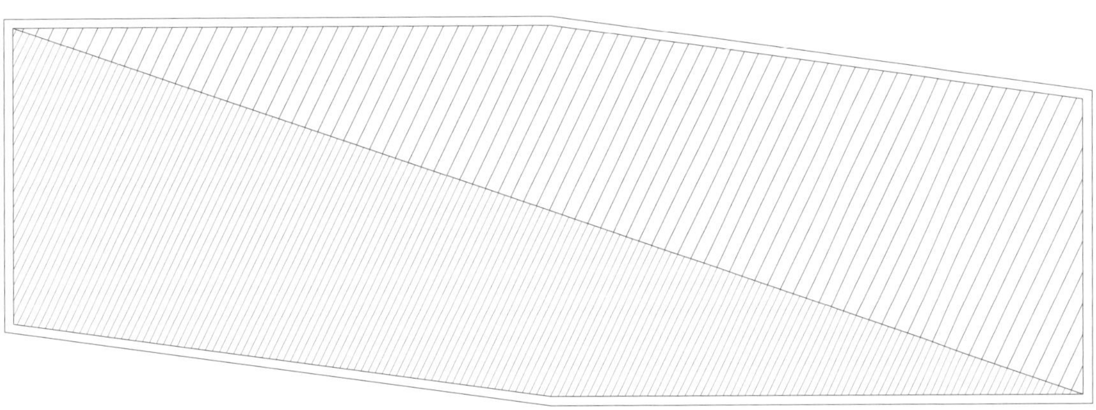

Roof plan

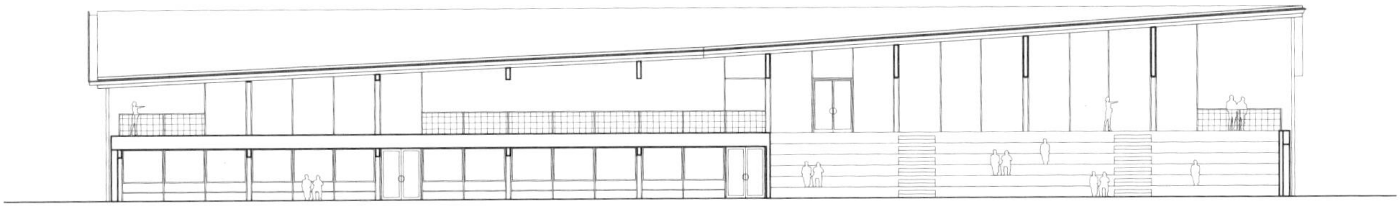

North elevation

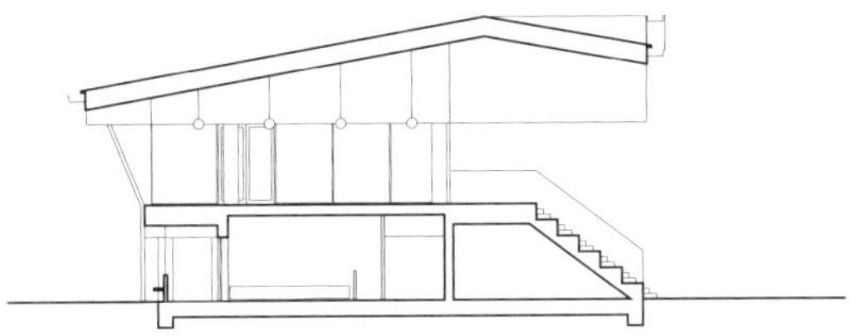

Section Aa

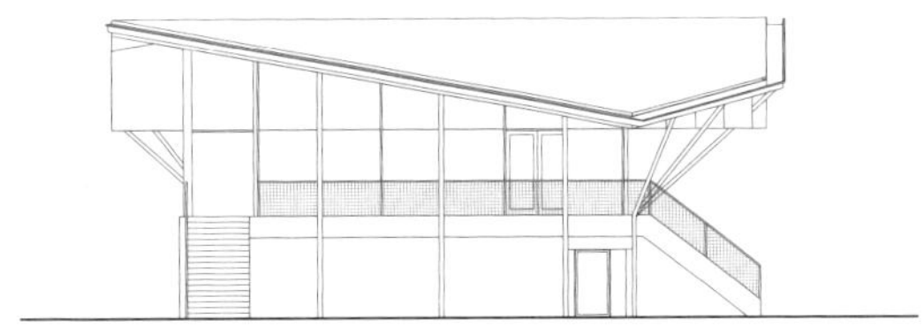

West elevation

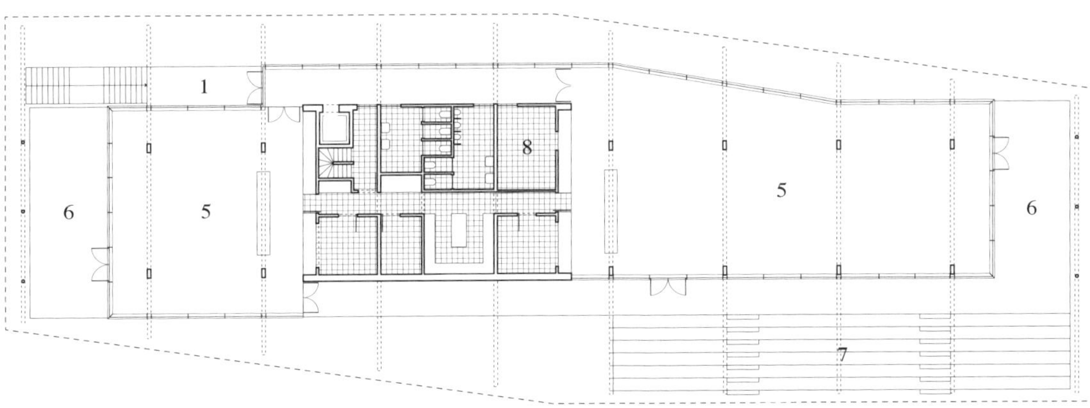

Floor 1

A

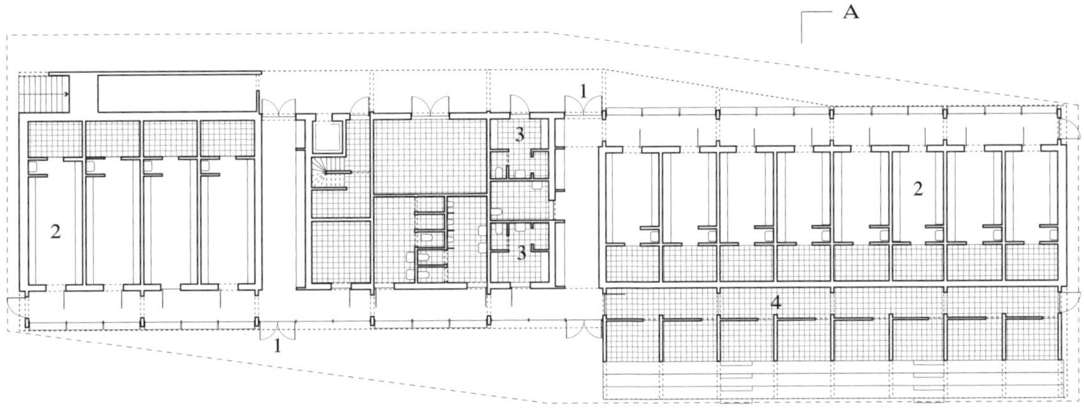

Floor 0

a

1 entrance
2 changing room
3 umpire's locker room
4 storage
5 cafeteria
6 terrace
7 grandstand
8 office

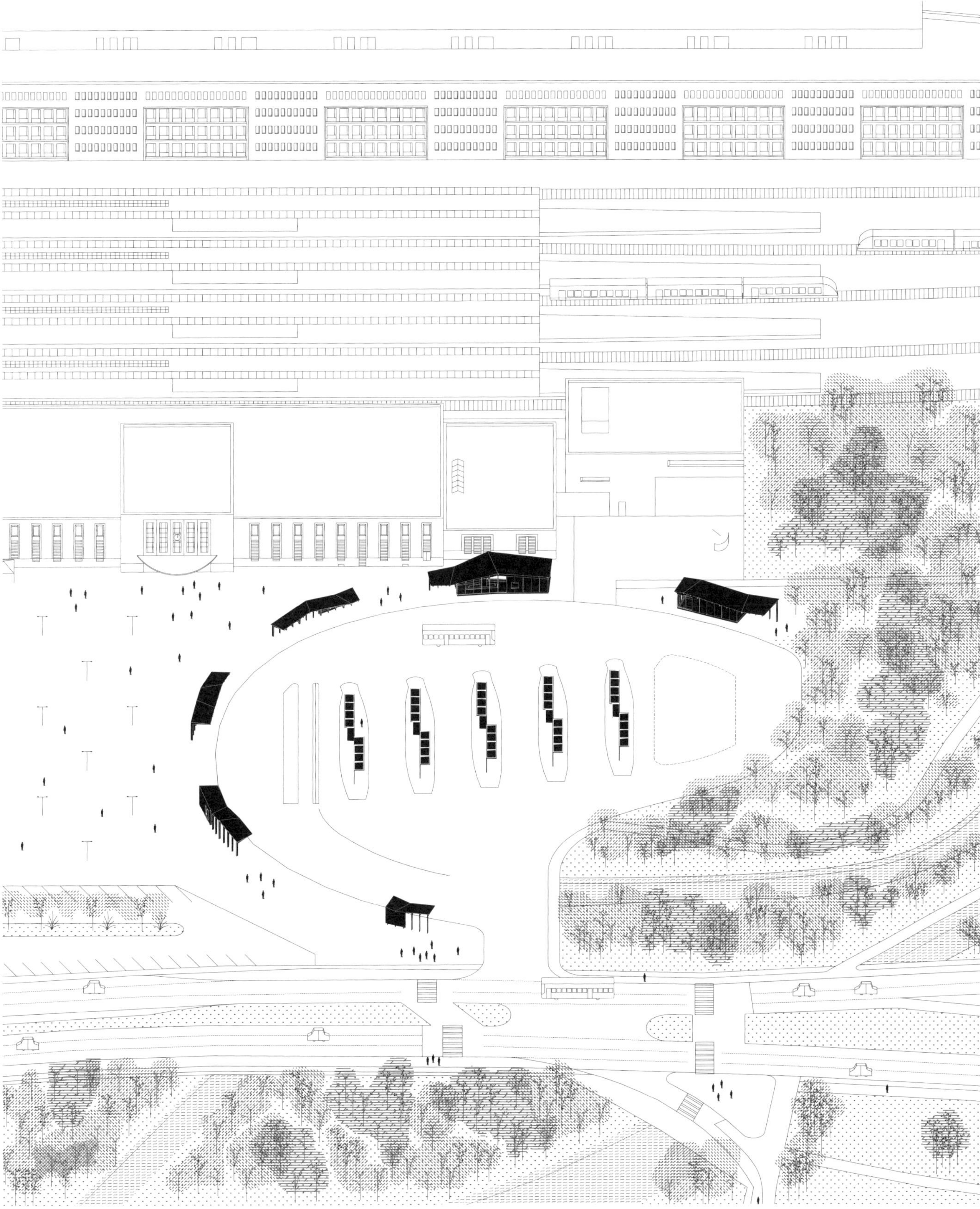

In 2012 the Flemish transport company De Lijn and the City of Bruges organized a competition for a new bus terminal on the square in front of the listed Art Deco station building. The assignment consisted in a series of stops for city and regional buses, a De Lijn shop, and a staff room. The different flows of users – buses, taxis, pedestrians and cyclists – also had to be better organized on the square.

URA won the competition with a design that united this diverse programme in a single gesture. Around the outermost turning circle of the buses, the architects designed a circular awning in thin steel plate at a height of about five metres: all functions are housed under this awning, which also helped to structure the station square.

After the competition phase, the design evolved towards six more distinct structures: four bus shelters for the regional buses, the De Lijn shop, and the staff room.

The six pavilions are built simply out of massive, welded steel plates painted in light blue. They vary in height but have been kept deliberately low so as not to impede the view of the station building and the city. Each pavilion is not only an abstract sculpture that offers shelter from the rain, wind and sun, but also a pragmatic structure that integrates all possible elements required for the bus terminal to function, such as seats, bins and signage.

As a series, the steel pavilions suggest a continuous movement around the five platforms for city buses in the middle of the square. These consist of white steel porticos with only a glass roof and a screen against the wind and rain.

URA chose to channel the diversity of user flows by relying on a simple figure that rests on a reduced use of material and minimalist detailing. [ldv]

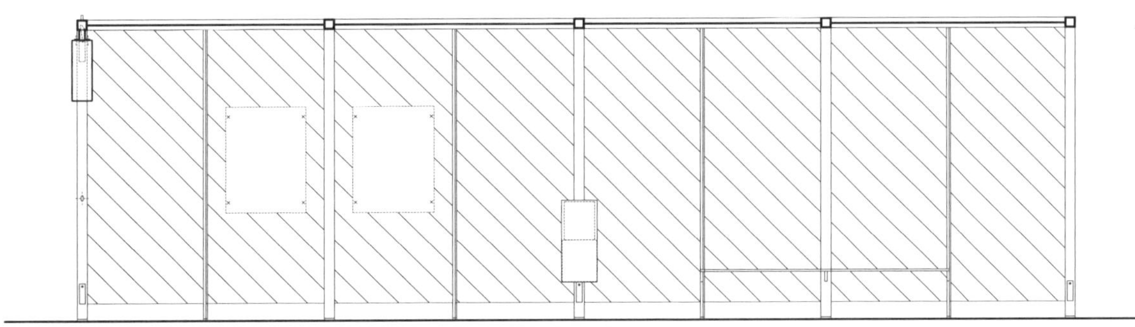

Elevation

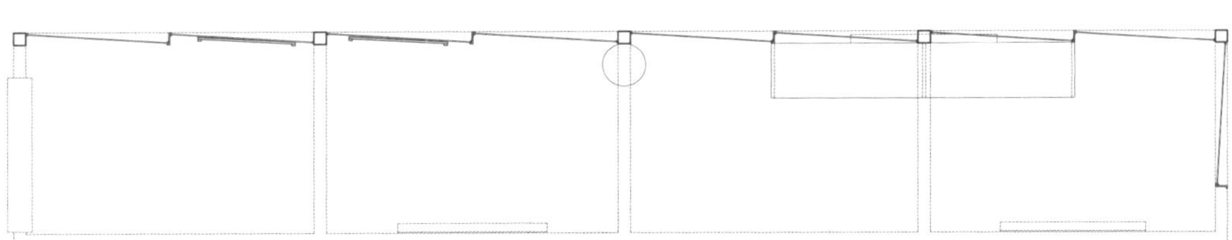

Floor 0

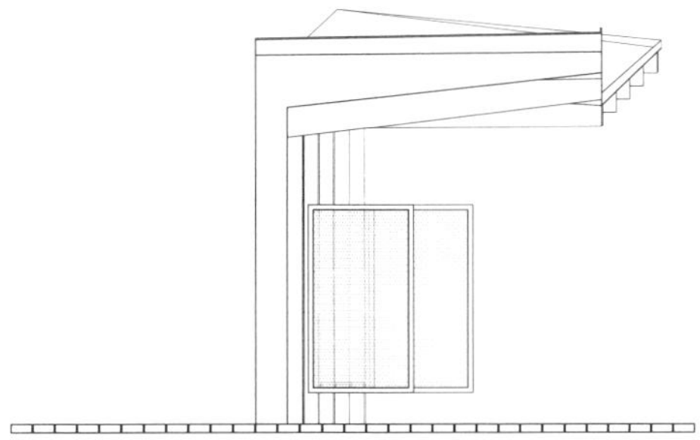

Section

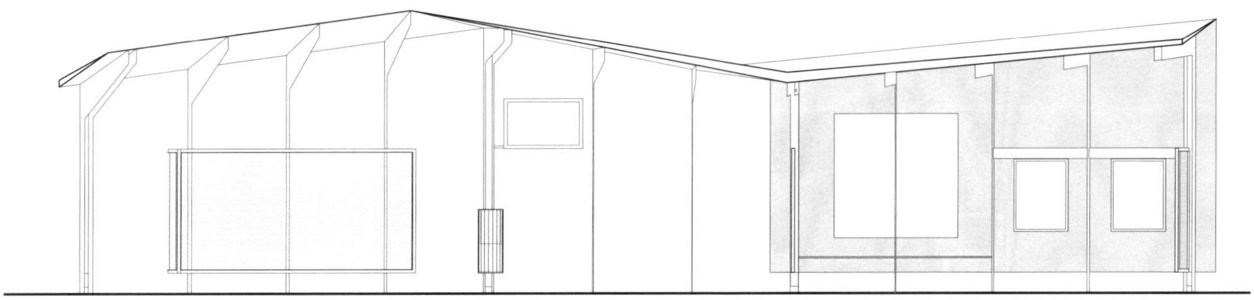

Elevation

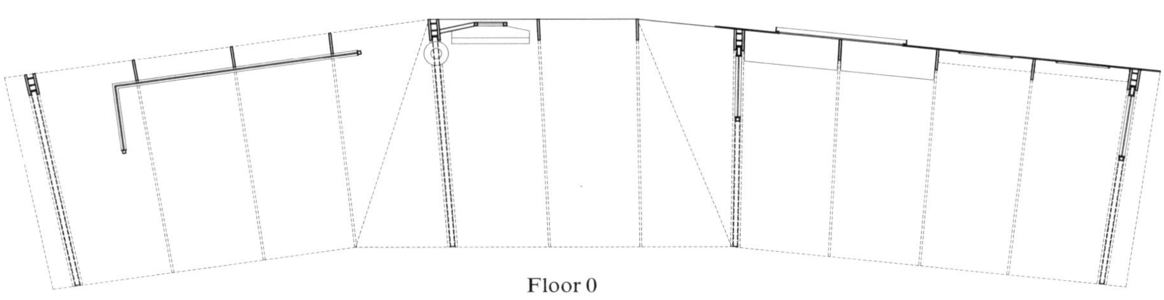

Floor 0

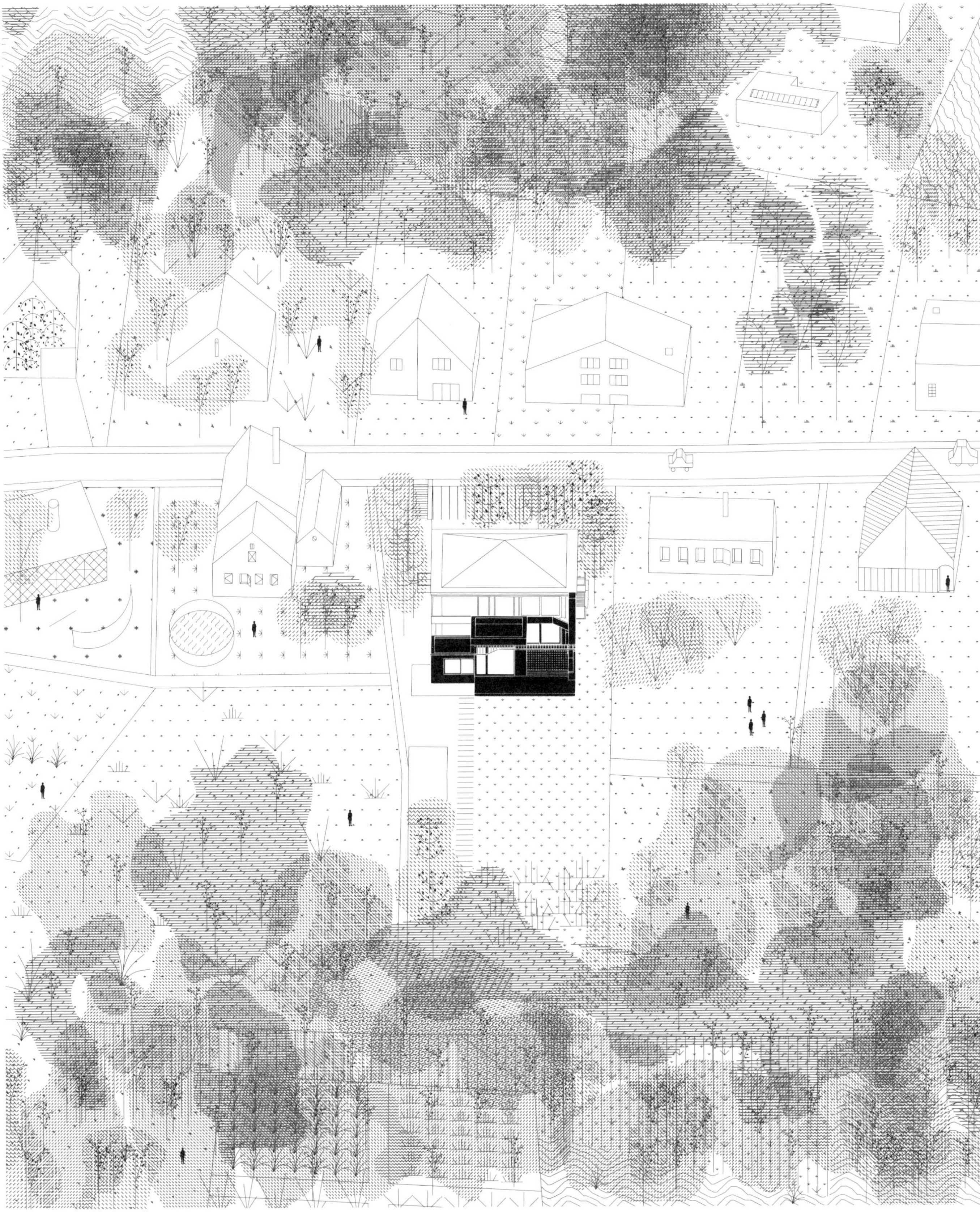

In a hilly landscape, on the border between the Brussels-Capital Region and the Pajottenland, URA was given carte blanche by friends of theirs. With its low ceilings and closed side walls, their ingenious architect's house from the 1970s needed to be expanded. At the rear, a banal veranda that had been added on was razed to make room for some sunlit rooms in which indoors and outdoors playfully interact.

The *promenade architecturale* from street to garden was extended. The existing house provides reason and direction, while the extension provides life, light and views. A black sliding door in the dining room ushers both residents and visitors to the back of the house. The former kitchen was transformed into a connecting space between old and new. The fact that it can be closed off ensures that the house and the extension can also be used separately from one another.

The dialectic of autonomy and continuity is specific to URA's approach. For the attentive eye, the intervention remains readable overall, but nowhere does it feel like a rupture. The module of the house itself served as a standard. Terrace tiles were preserved and form an outdoor room, delimited by the existing barbecue and a new outdoor bench, built with the same bricks. A steel canopy starts here, filtering the light and connecting the different volumes, each with their own cladding.

Fibre cement façade panels were used for the kitchen-kiosk and simply run on inside, up to the kitchen cupboards. A multifunctional kitchen unit made of wood and composite material ensures the transition to the final point and heart of the *promenade*: a square, wainscoted dining corner with views indoors and outdoors. The wooden table with a black-steel frame was designed by URA with the idea of accommodating a range of people in different circumstances. [fc]

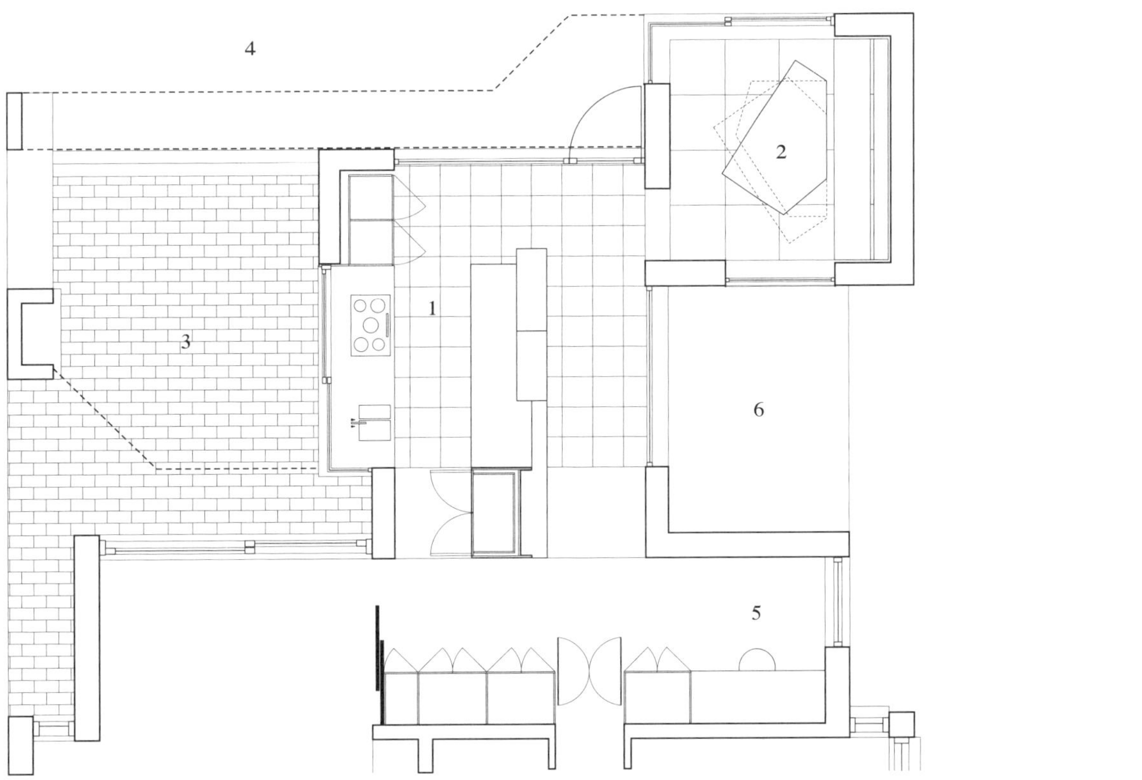

Floor 0

1 kitchen
2 cabanon
3 patio
4 terrace
5 office
6 botanical garden

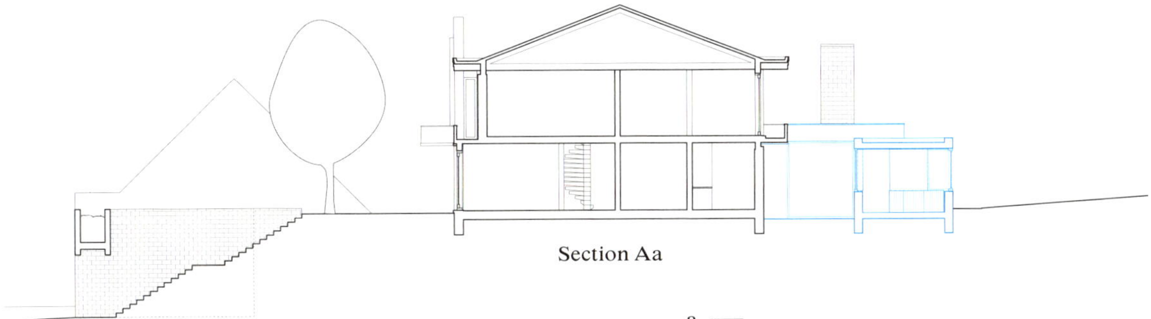

Section Aa

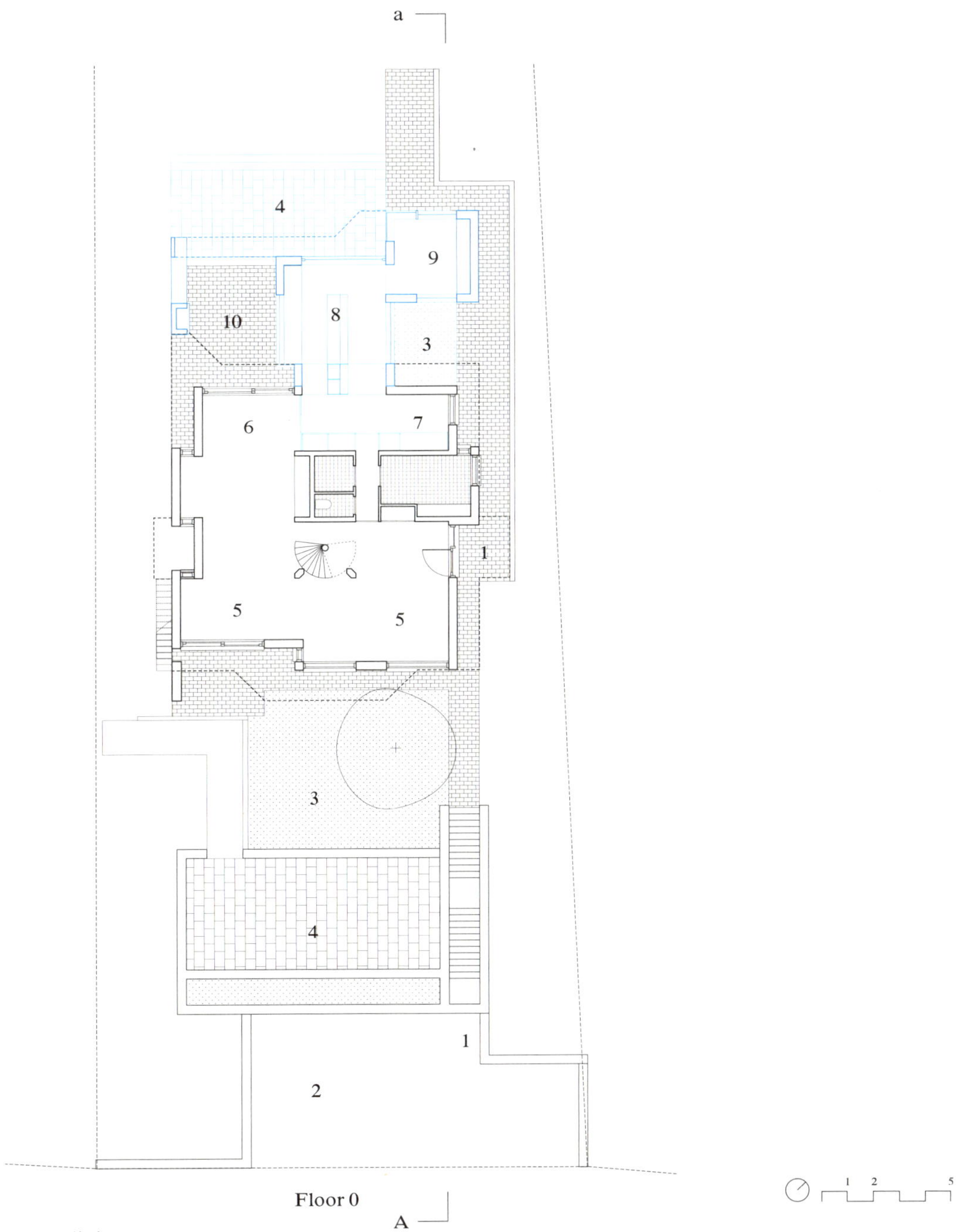

Floor 0

1 entrance
2 driveway
3 botanical garden
4 terrace
5 living room
6 dining room
7 office
8 kitchen
9 cabanon
10 patio

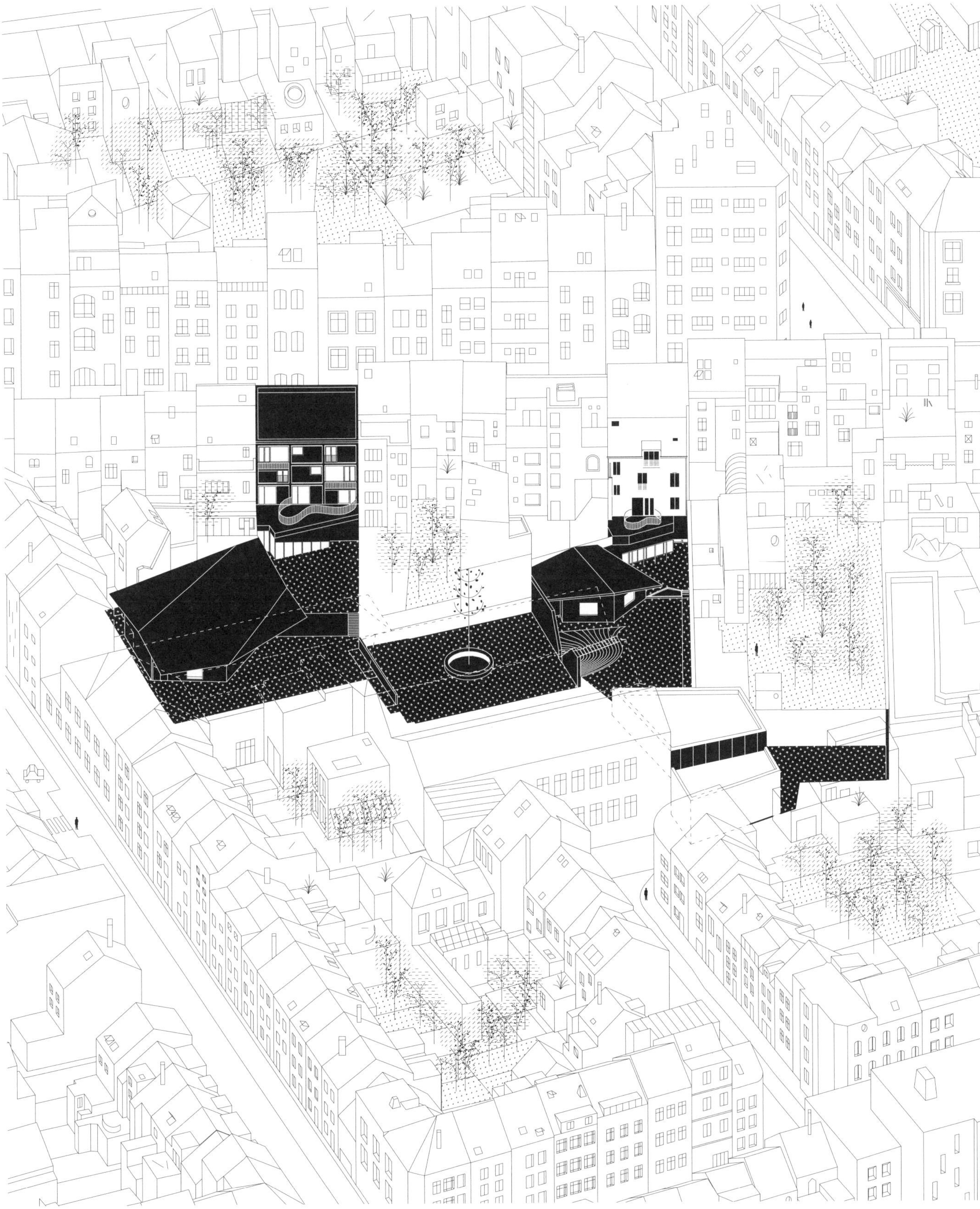

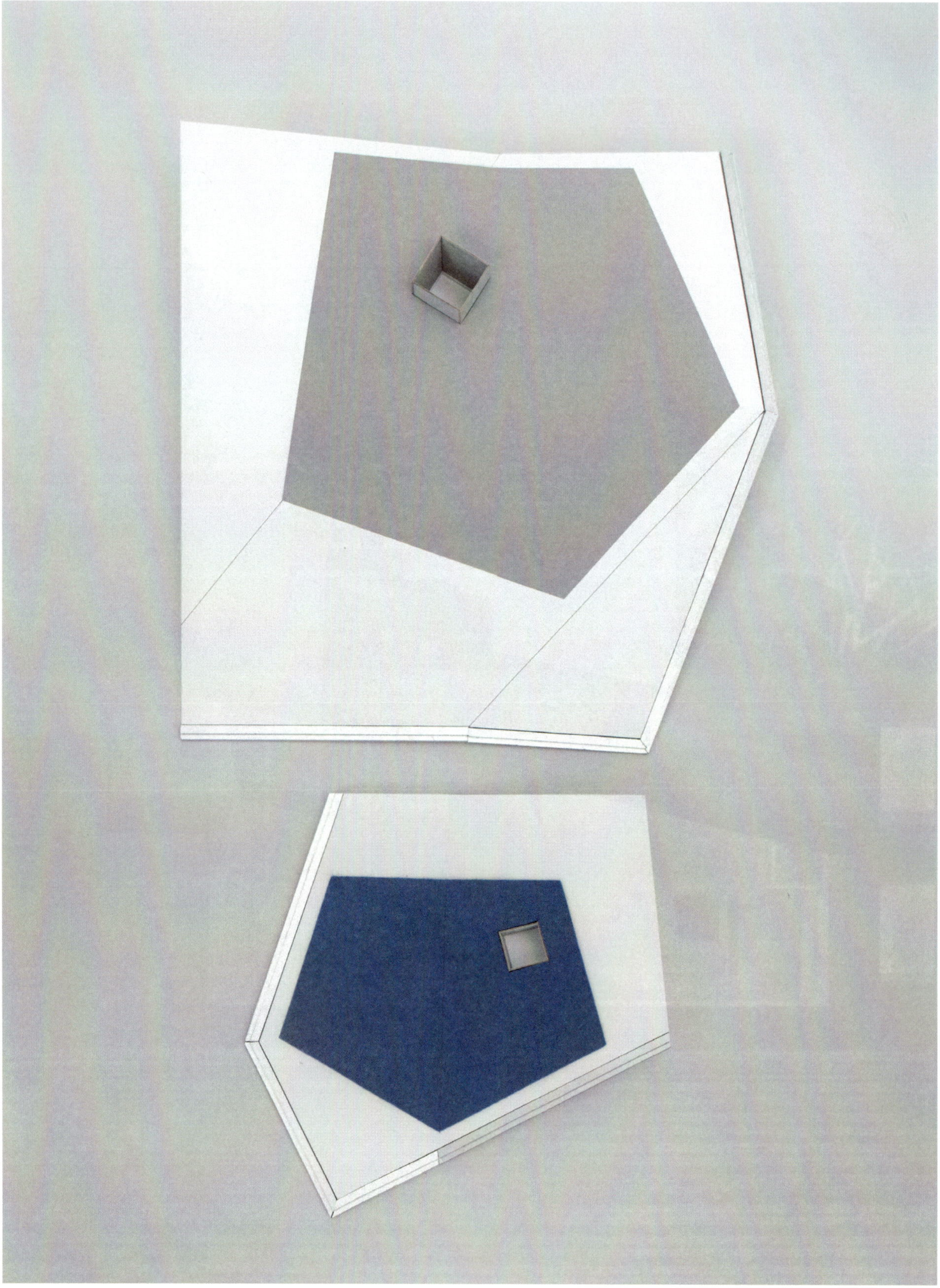

On an introverted urban plot on Avenue d'Auderghem in the municipality of Etterbeek, an intergenerational pool is currently being built with diligence. Social housing, crèche, auditorium, multipurpose foyer, meeting centre, toy library: loose ends are being tied together and connected with the neighbouring school and environment. The urban acupuncture of BXL100 is here becoming a reality. URA won the competition in the context of a sustainable neighbourhood contract.

It is with kid gloves that the architects are intervening in the existing situation. Demolition is being limited, building and topography restructured. The trapeze-shaped wall incision and the fan-shaped crèche and auditorium provide maximum openness and connection with the formal diversity of garden walls and differences in level.

On the western plot border, a former boules club, once designed by Pierre Blondel, has been tactfully converted into a toy library. An indented garden path departs from here – or ends here, depending on your point of view – in the direction of Avenue d'Auderghem. A former house, on the one hand, and a new construction, on the other, provide access to the interior area. The ground floor has been kept deliberately porous to draw in the city and to draw the garden out into the city.

The house is being transformed into a meeting place for young parents, and the new construction includes a crèche, social housing and access to the auditorium with a multipurpose foyer on the ground floor. The foyer, the project's connecting centre, ties the different spaces and levels to each other with the help of some interior and exterior windows.

The concrete shell of the auditorium has been left visible on the ceiling. For acoustic reasons, the walls have been covered with blue felt. Together with the discreet overhead lighting, the royal blue heightens the sense of safety in the heart of this city in the city. [fc]

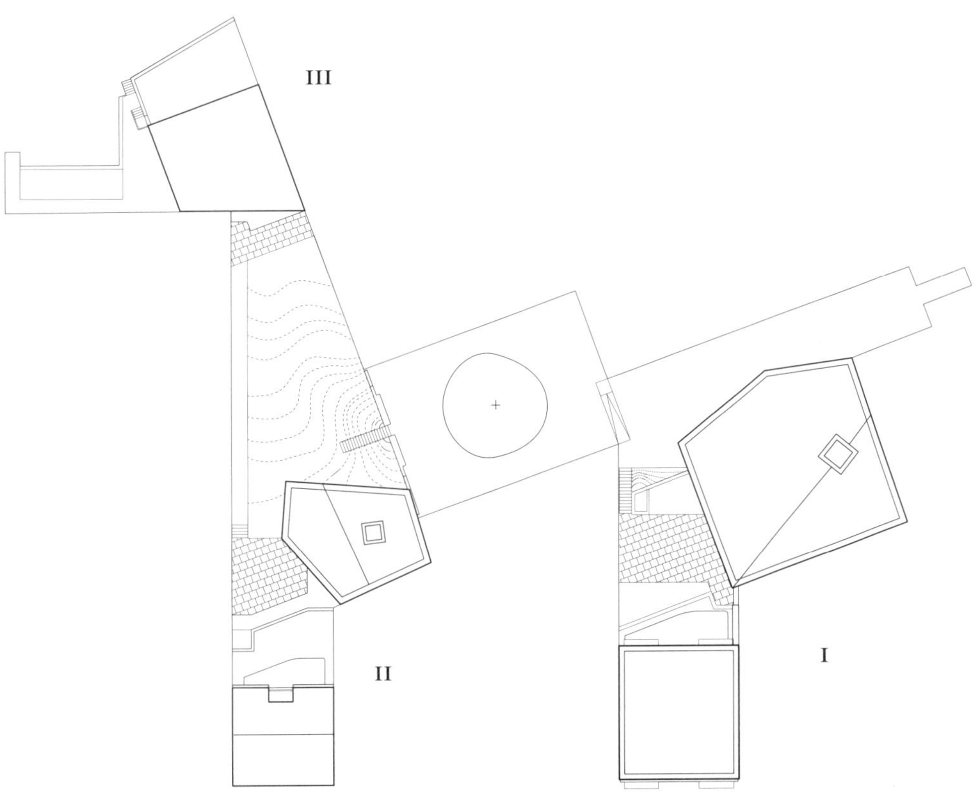

I Music pavilion and crèche
II Family house
III Toy library

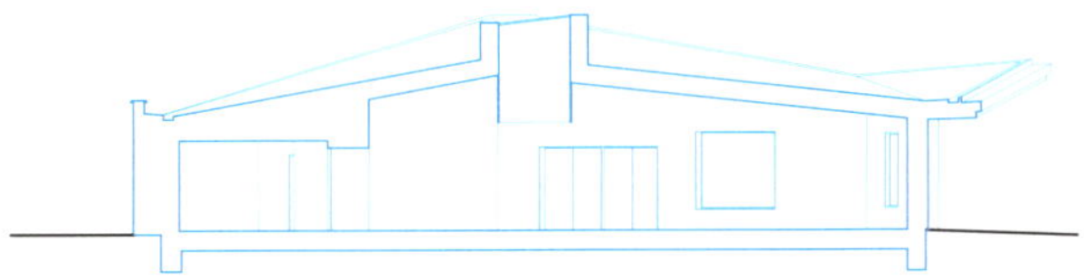

Section Aa

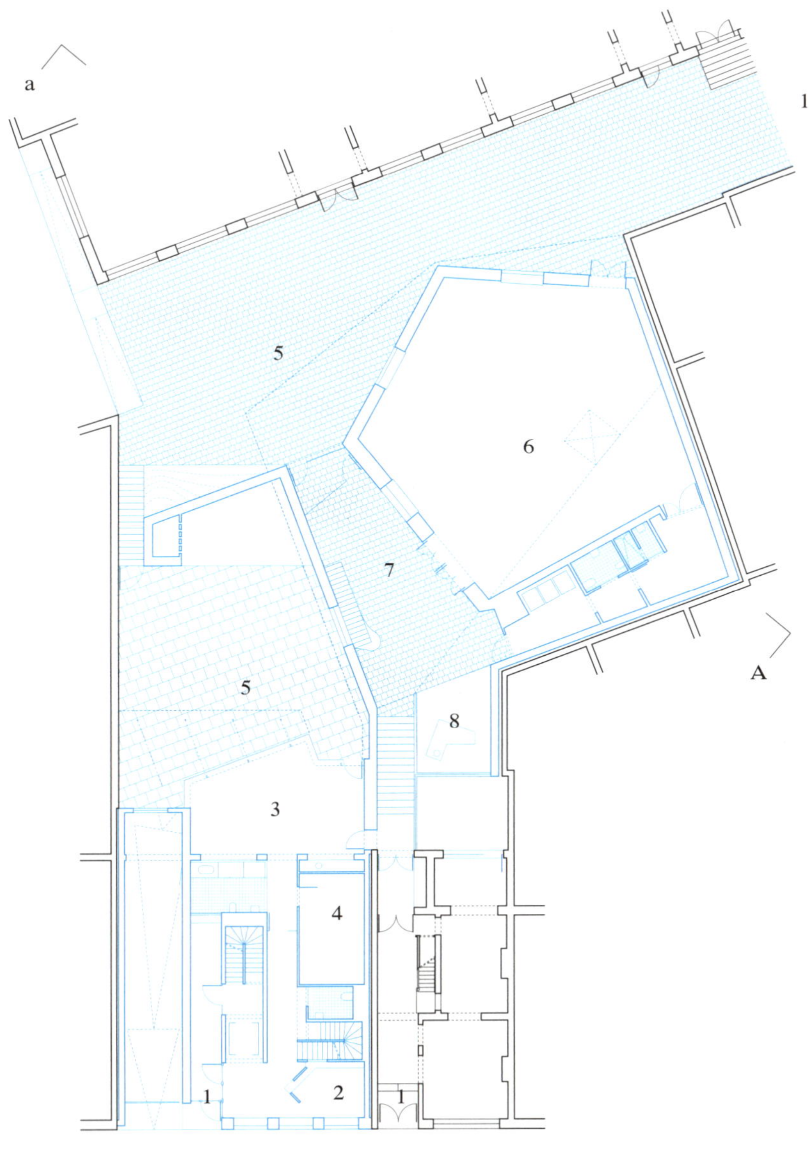

Floor 0

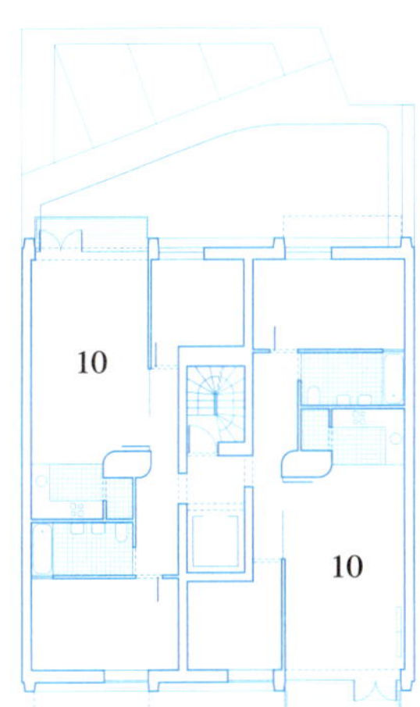

Floor 2

1 entrance
2 reception
3 play area
4 bedroom
5 playground
6 auditorium
7 foyer
8 bar
9 patio
10 apartment

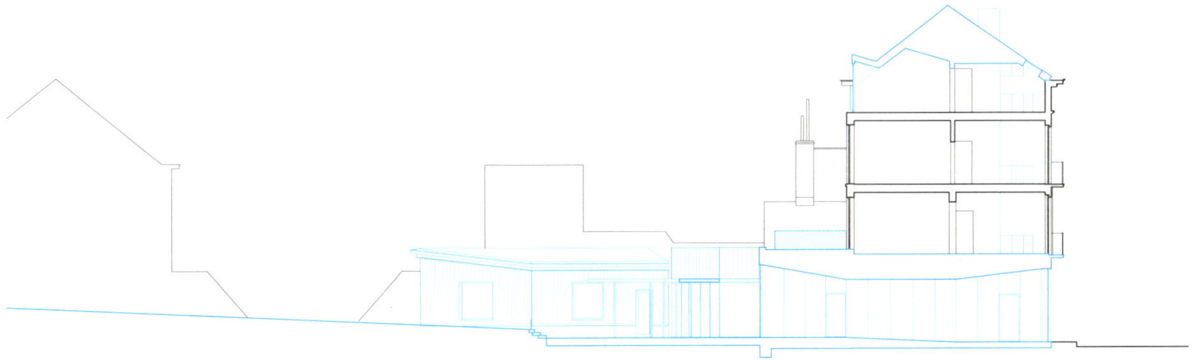

Section Bb

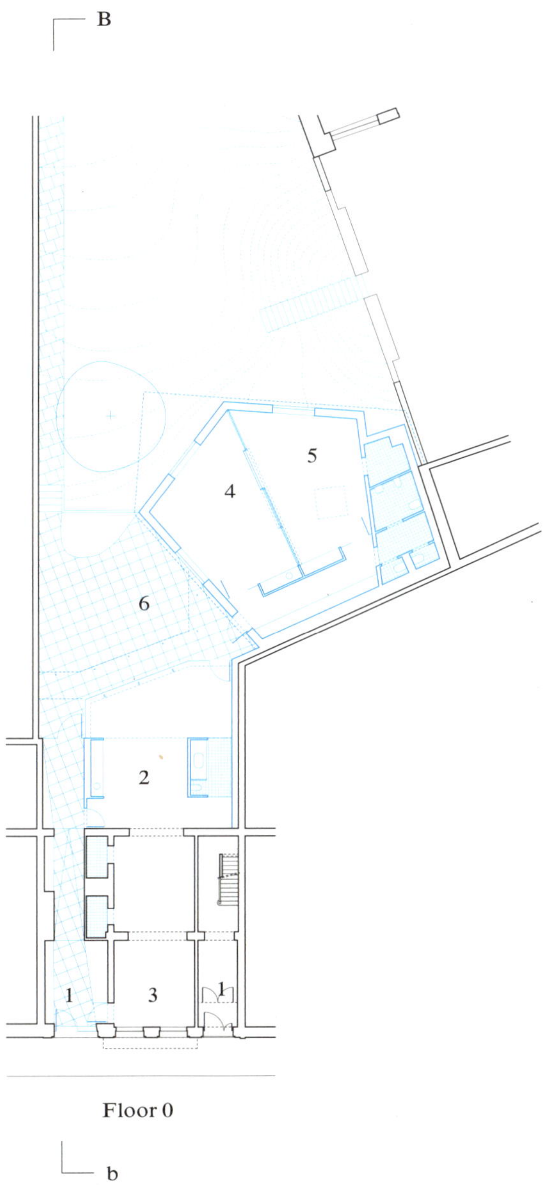

Floor 0

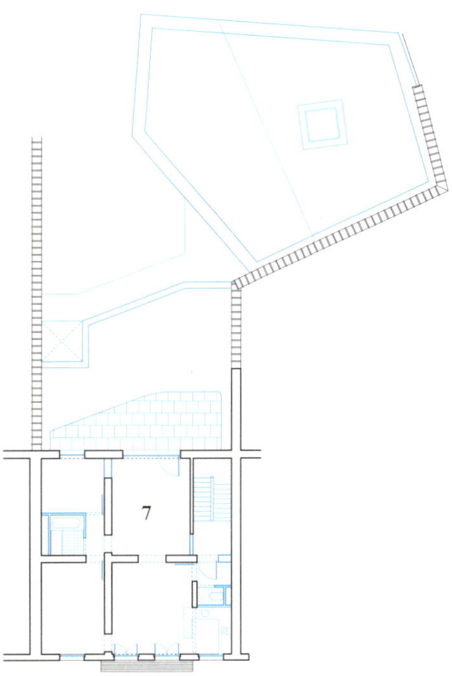

Floor 1

1 entrance
2 play area
3 sleeping room
4 family room
5 workshop
6 terrace
7 apartment

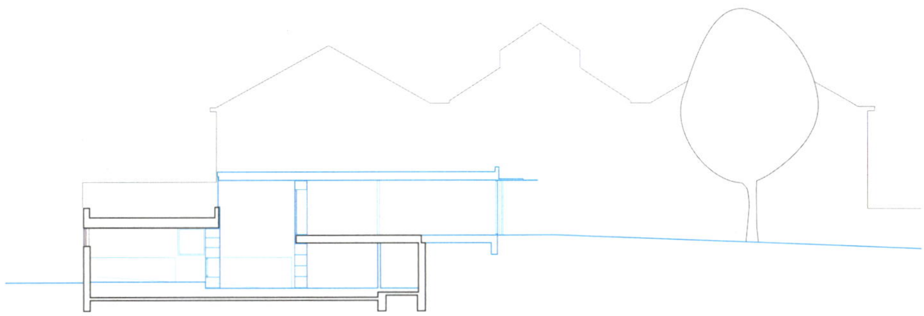

Section Cc

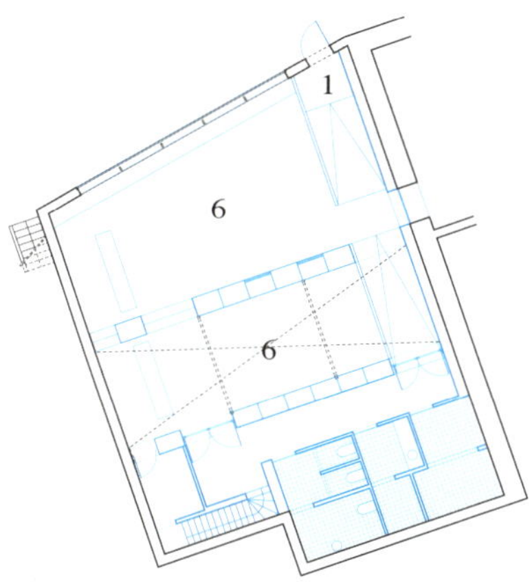

Floor street

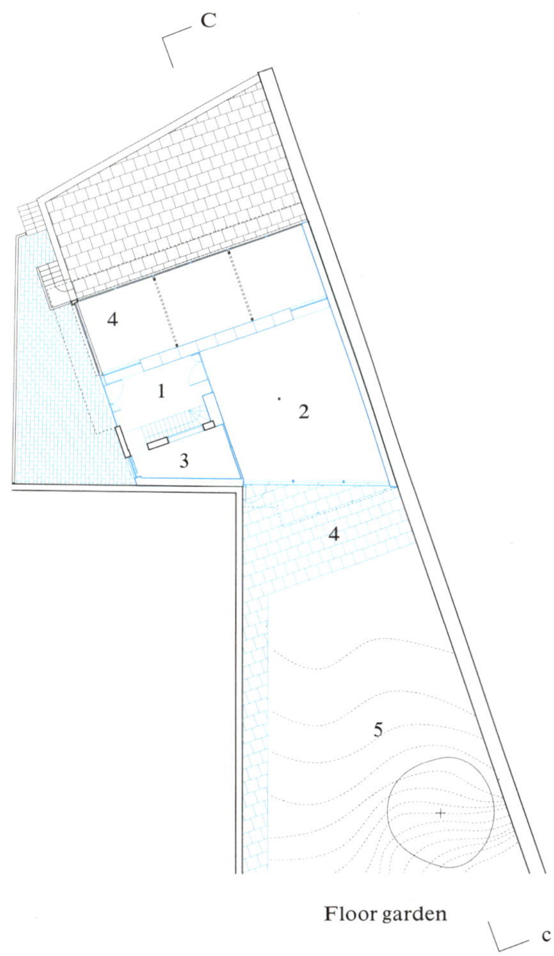

Floor garden

1 entrance
2 workshop
3 office
4 terrace
5 garden
6 toy library

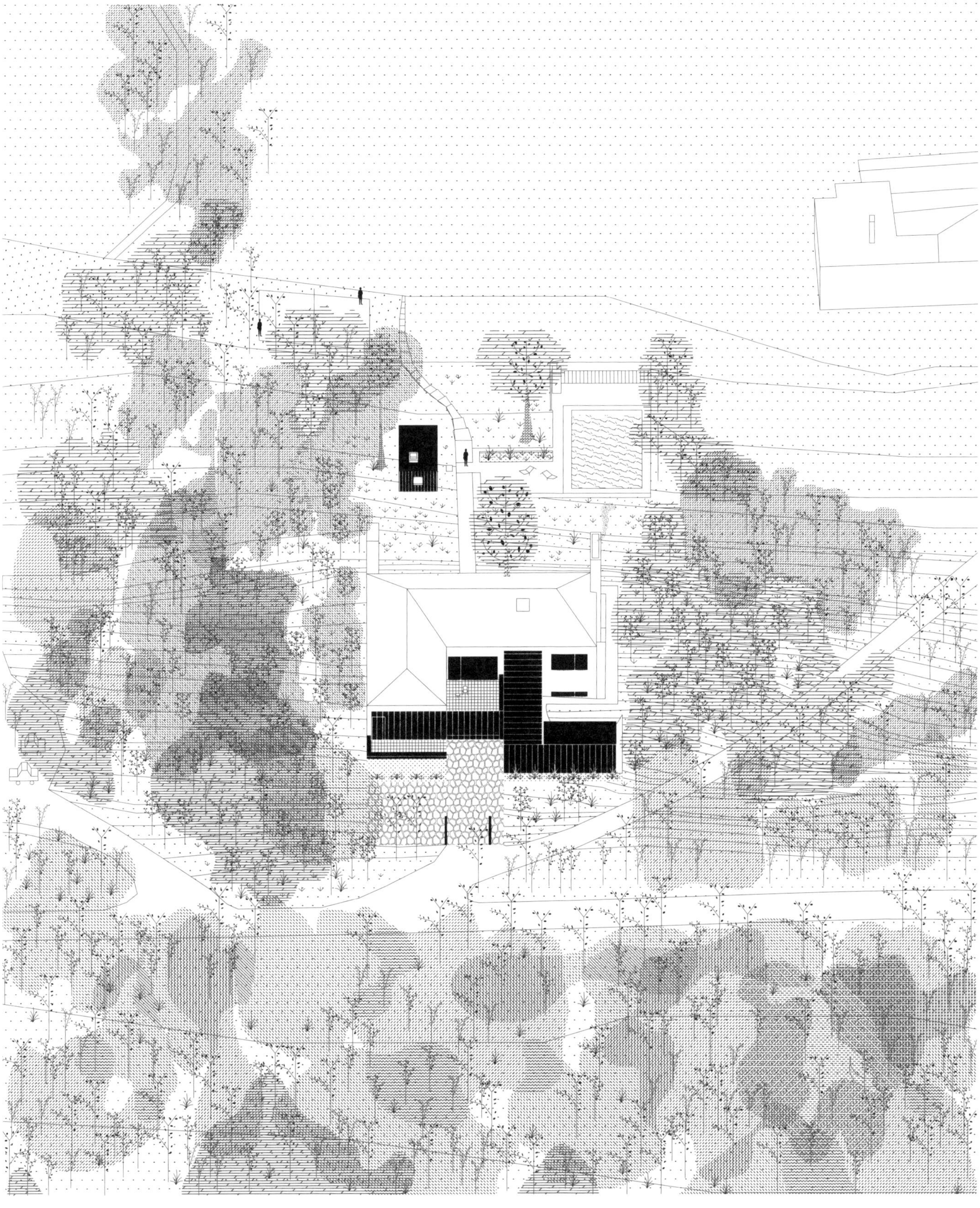

After visiting a house in Ypres, an architecture enthusiast took his chances with the same architects. His 1960s holiday home in Heuvelland had to be brought back to life and adapted to a permanent residence. Armed with the reference of Aalto's Maison Louis Carré outside Paris, the assignment was clear as can be: 'Give me my house back!'

'My house' referred to the inherent soul of the place. Engineer Hubert Van Kerckhove built the holiday home for a cattle-feed manufacturer beside his own home on the Kemmelberg. *Pour vivre heureux, vivons cachés*: although the views towards the French agricultural and industrial horizon are spectacular, the house was nestled almost invisibly against the slope of the hill. A first design dating from 1961 was considered too progressive by the initial commissioners. The sloping roof, a later addition, further enhanced the absence of the present architecture.

Accommodating the environment and assignment, URA set to work to bring the house to a state which it had in fact never been in. Contradictions rich in contrast were avoided, while changes were introduced and implemented subtly. Materials such as yellow bricks outside and De Coene wainscoting inside were simply taken up again in order to work on the liveability of the house.

The owner had 17 holes in mind to make the holiday house inhabitable. New wall openings ensure porosity, but can also be closed up again. The abundant use of mirrors and seamlessly built-in (cupboard) doors further ensures a labyrinthine sense of liveability.

A few carefully conceived outdoor places further anchor the house in the Kemmelberg. The former carport was turned into the master bedroom. A steel canopy divides the front garden into four areas, of which two sheltered outdoor spaces that attenuate the point of contact between street and house. The front door was moved to the front and enlarged in order to let more light into the hall. The architects resisted the temptation to emphasize immediately the almost Bruegelian, fictive-looking landscape. The panoramic views can only be perceived in the heart of the house itself, e.g. beside the original fireplace. [fc]

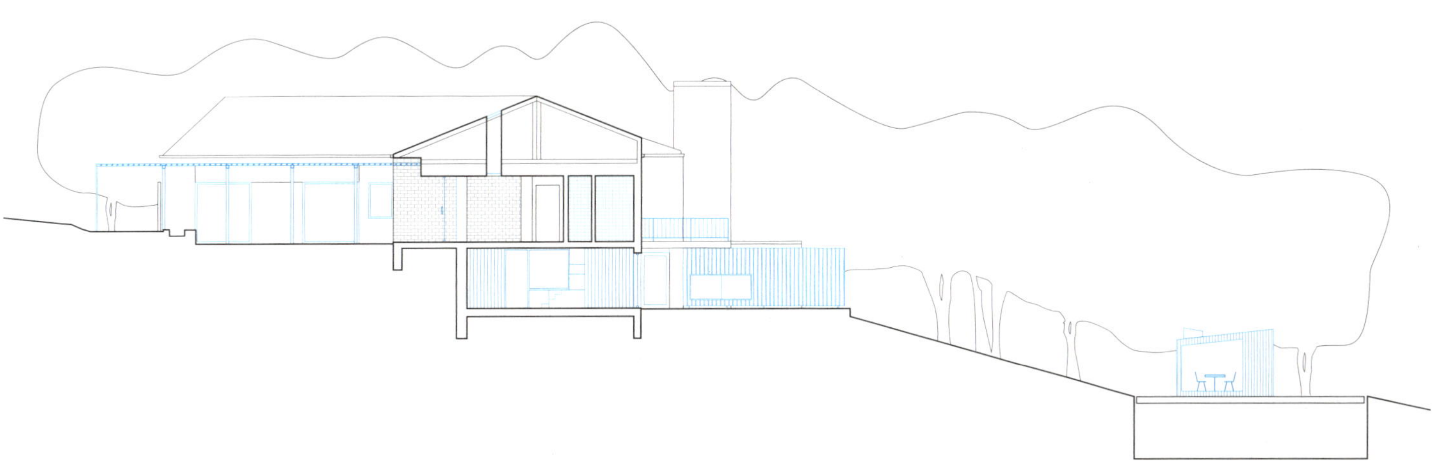

Section Aa

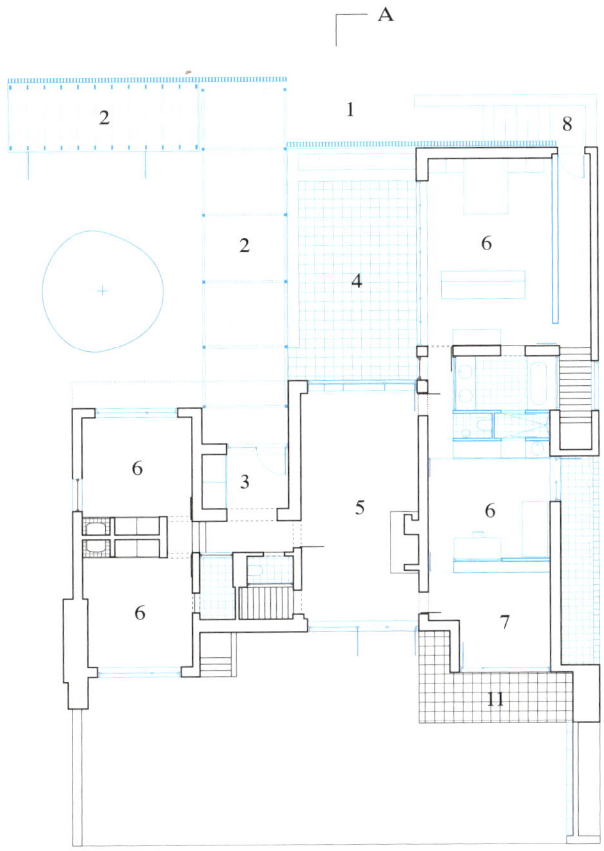

Floor 1

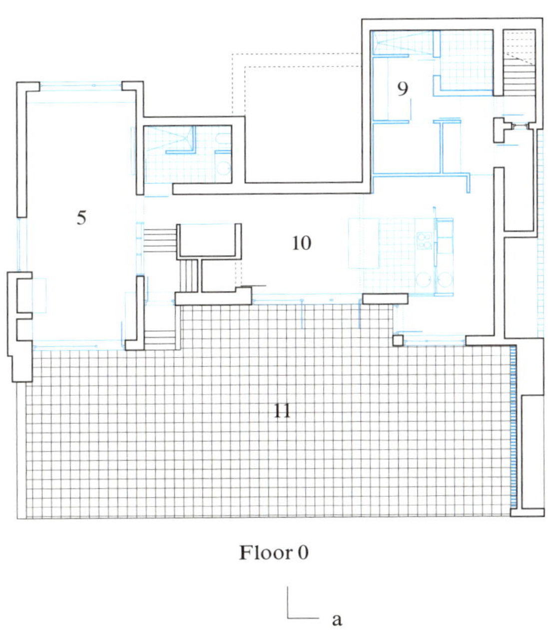

Floor 0

1 entrance
2 portico
3 vestibule
4 courtyard
5 living room
6 bedroom
7 library
8 service entrance
9 sauna
10 dining room
11 terrace

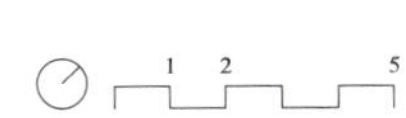

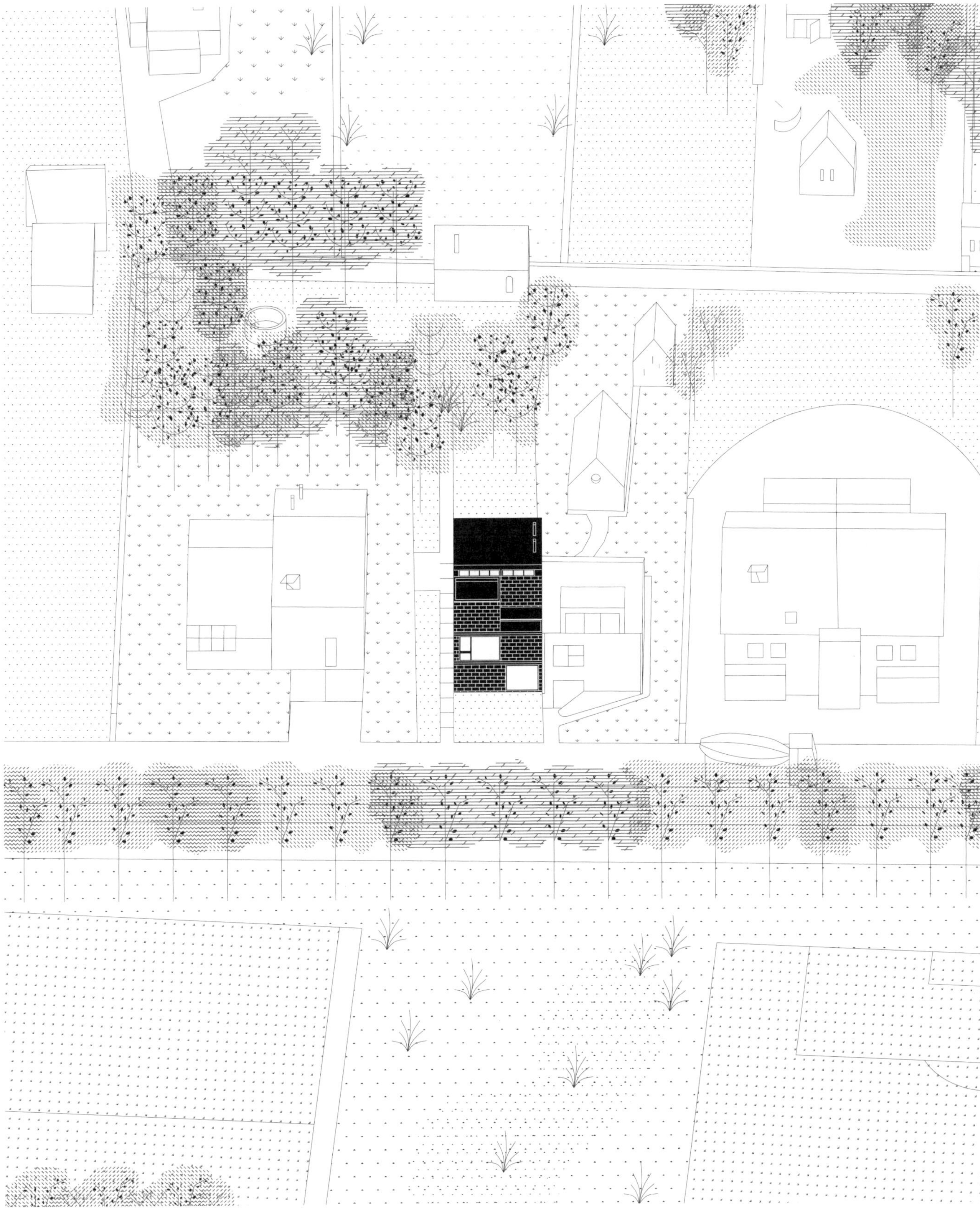

Beigem (Grimbergen)

In a typical residential area from the 1960s, URA built a new semi-detached house for a couple with two children. The house had to be connected to the home of the neighbours and had to meet a number of urban-planning regulations. The most decisive of these were a sloping roof and the height of the cornice. These meant that the houses in this neighbourhood had a dug-in garage, only one main floor, and bedrooms in a dormer.

After negotiations, the urban-planning authorities approved a reinterpretation of the dormer, allowing URA to create three full-fledged floors. Starting from the highest point of the cornice, the architects designed a compact house around a staircase with landings and branches to floors and delimited spaces of varying sizes and heights. The open kitchen downstairs and the first-floor living room, which is higher than it is wide, offer extensive views of the garden and the orchard behind it through the fully glazed rear façade. Through a small window in the side wall, the architects drew natural light into the central staircase and the bathroom next to the parents' bedroom on the first floor. The walk through the house with ever-changing views and perspectives finally leads you to the children's smaller bedrooms, a hobby room in the recess and a south-facing roof terrace on the top floor. Each storey has areas in which to spend time together but also rooms in which to isolate oneself.

On the first and second floors, a concrete wall, poured on site, ensures the span from side wall to side wall. It forms the central buttress for all the floors and landings that connect to it. The concrete slab shows the traces of the plank formwork and has otherwise been left bare. The interior walls in cinder blocks were left unplastered and only painted white. They contrast with the refined finish of the smaller, intimate spaces, such as the gold-painted entrance hall and the bathroom with yellow faïence tiles.

The sturdy yellow-brick volume is a low-energy house, a precursor of passive buildings. The architects used the thickness of the outer walls to create niches in it. In the outer walls, the thickness of the floors is defined by double stretcher courses at the same height as the horizontal lines in the adjoining house. [ed]

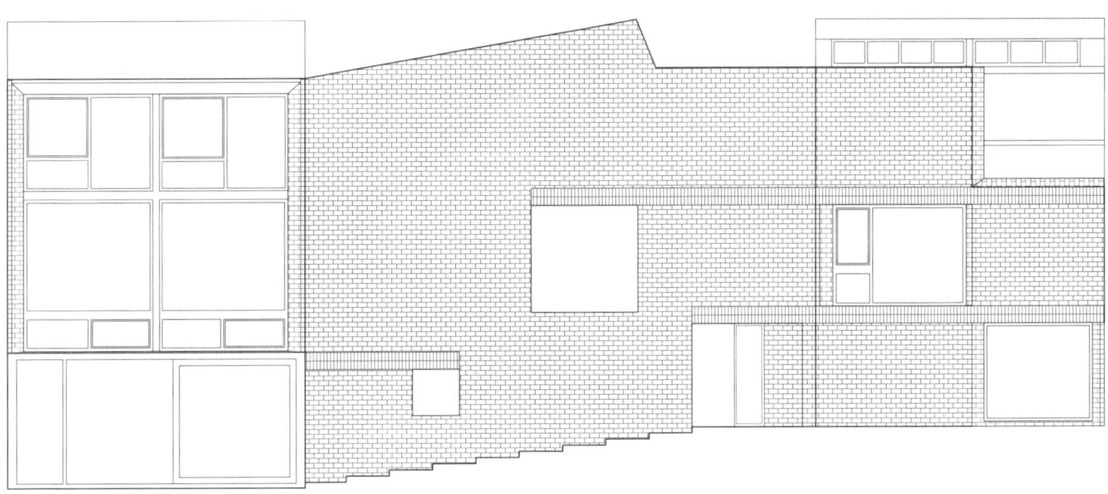

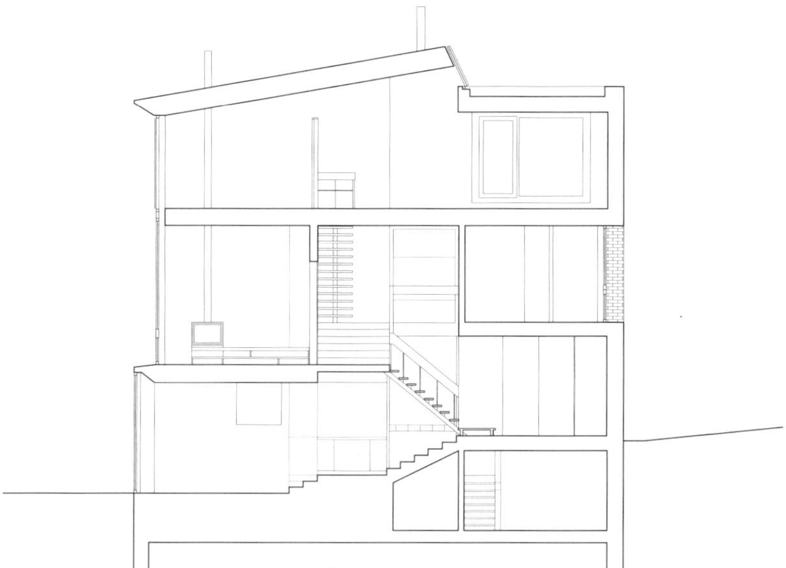

Section Aa

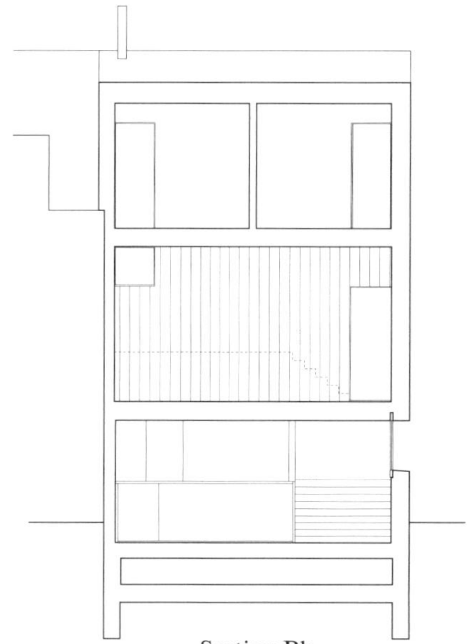

Section Bb

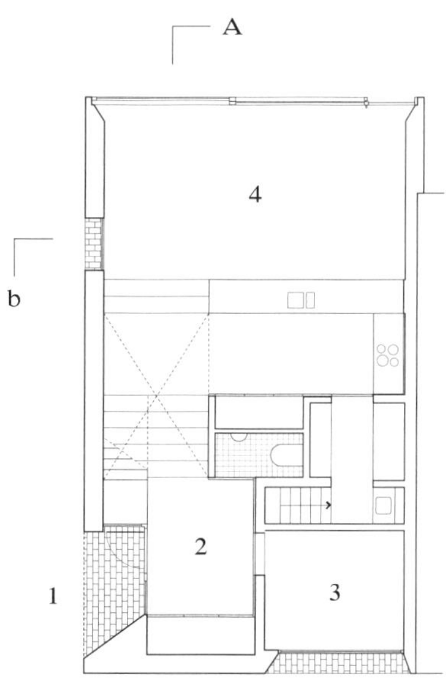

Floor 0

a

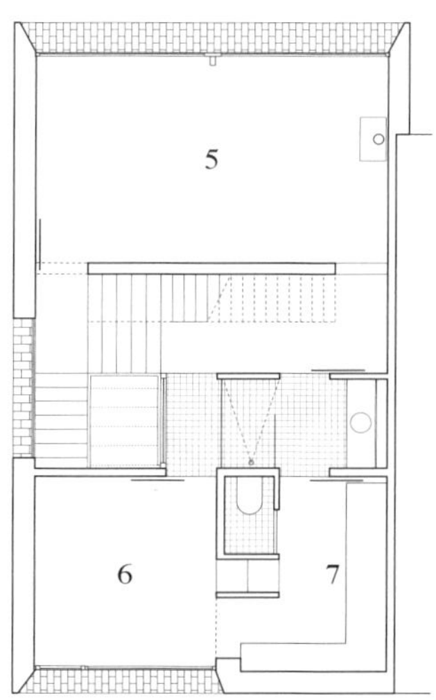

Floor 1

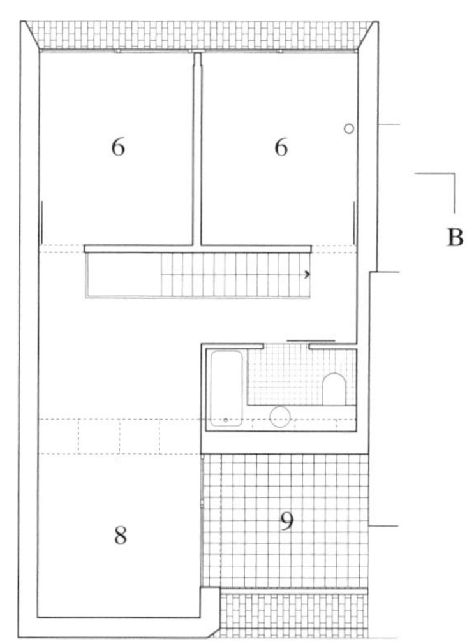

Floor 2

1 entrance
2 vestibule
3 office
4 dining room
5 living room
6 bedroom
7 dressing room
8 workshop
9 roof terrace

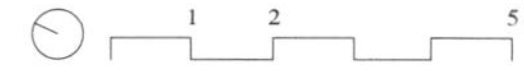

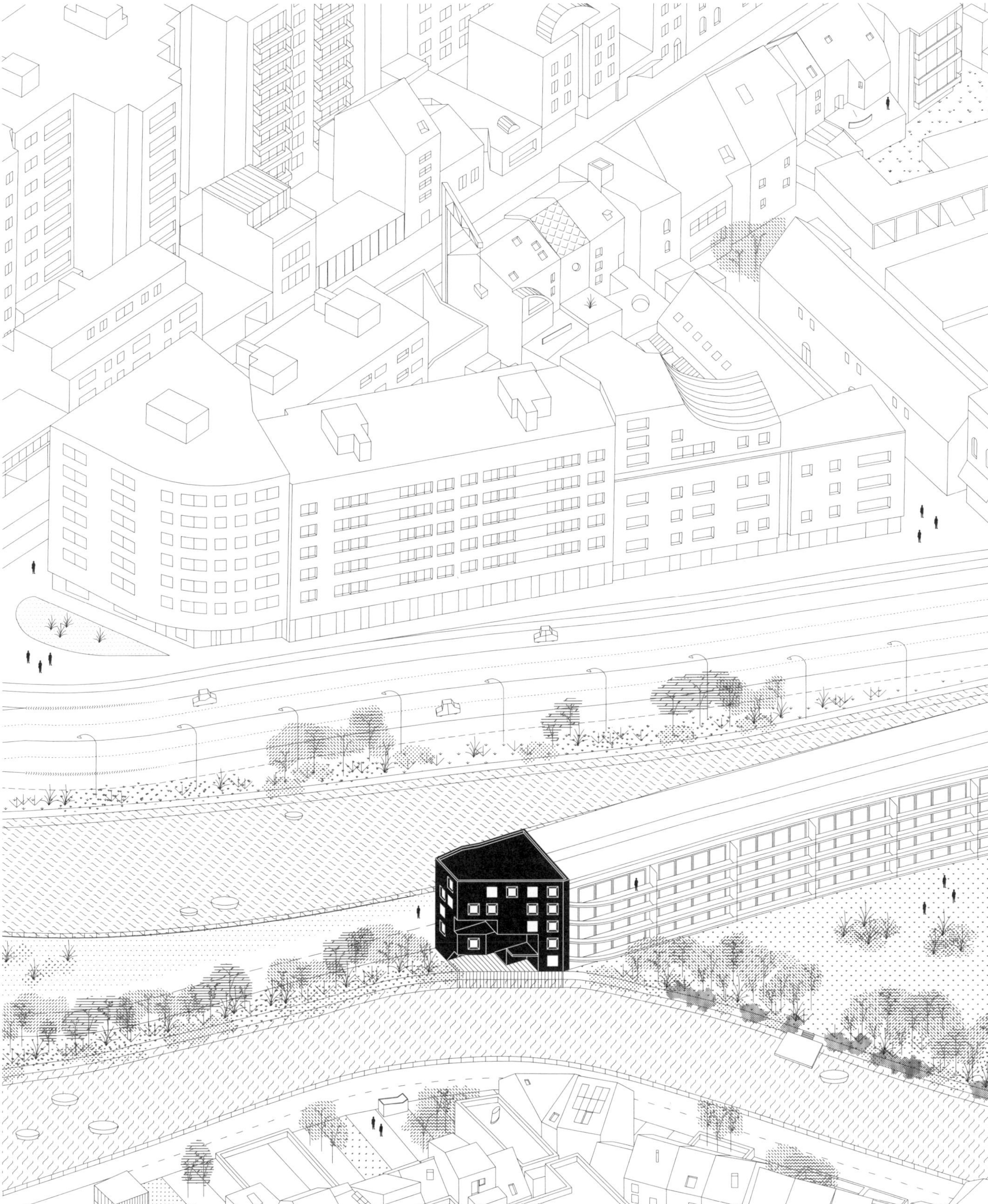

At the end of a plot on the Pynaert quay in Ledeberg, where the Metzeler rubber factory used to be, URA built three stacked dwellings. The corner building is the final piece of a housing development on the edge of Ghent's inner city, located between two arms of the river Scheldt and clearly visible from the parallel flyover.

Whether by motorists, skippers, cyclists or walkers, the building is perceptible at various speeds from various angles and various heights. That is why URA decided to place a building with three front façades on the unbuilt, triangular plot. The architects started out from a massive volume that they hollowed out, carved into and folded. The volumetric exercise led to a tangible sculpture in natural stone that stands out against the banality of the adjacent apartment building and asserts its own presence.

To ensure that attention is focused on the monolithic character, all window openings are of the same size (1.80 x 1.80 m). However, URA introduced some variation. The oblique interior frames each determine a different viewing direction. On the street side, a fold juts forward to create more views over the city.

To offer each of the three dwellings similar qualities in terms of urban views and exposure to sun and water, URA gave a different interpretation to the urbanistic prescriptions in force: instead of vertical, ground-based dwellings, the architects suggested three horizontally stacked duplexes with different levels that each offer a different view onto the surroundings. The unit on the ground floor has a garden, while the units on the first and second floors have either a walled-in terrace or a patio with a view of the water.

Each unit retains its own private front door at street level and has a bicycle storage and either a garage or an open parking space. Except for a massive shaft that anchors the building in the ground, the base remains open. Shortcuts and perspectives offer views from the street onto the collective terrace on the side of the water. [ed]

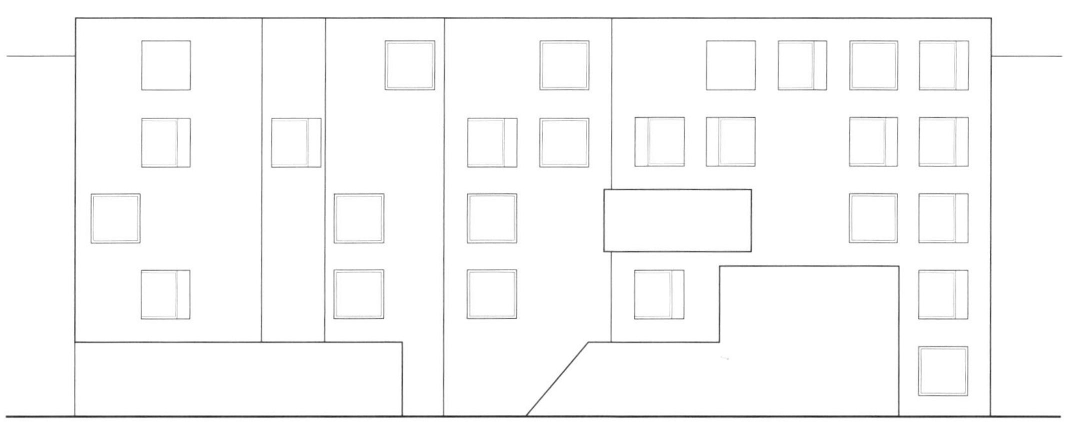

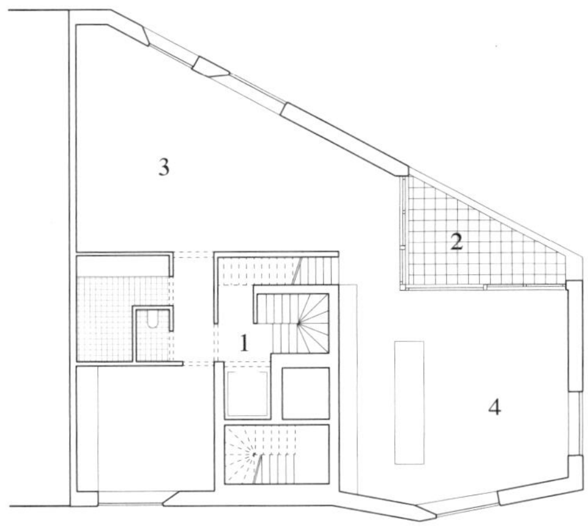

Floor 2

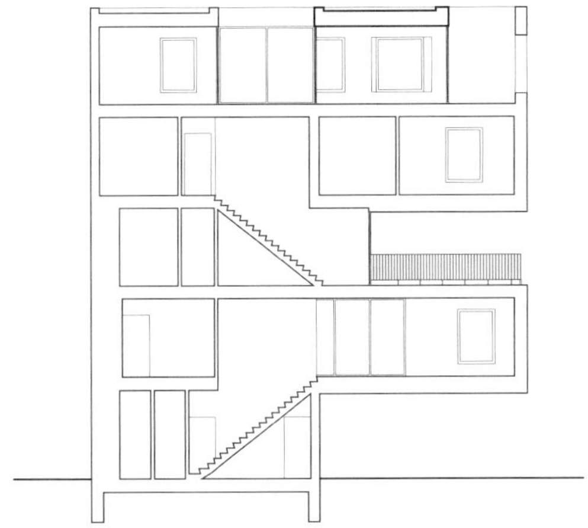
Section Aa

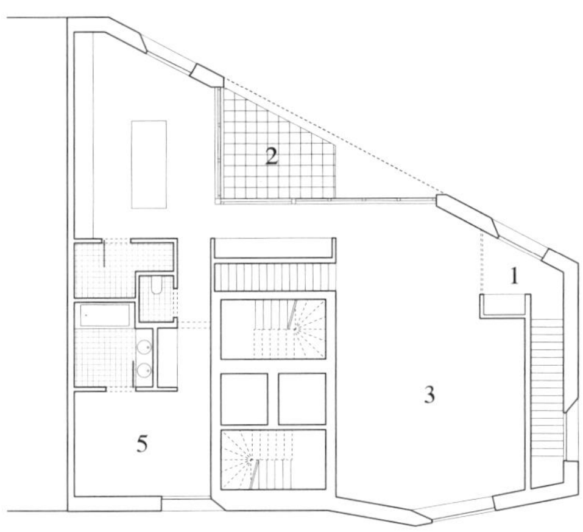

Floor 1

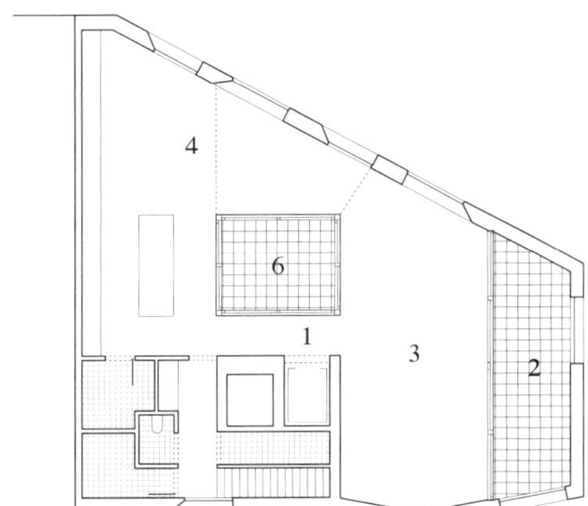

Floor 4

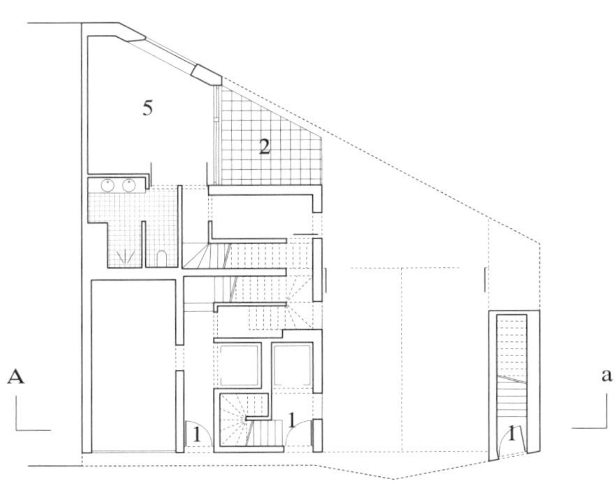

Floor 0

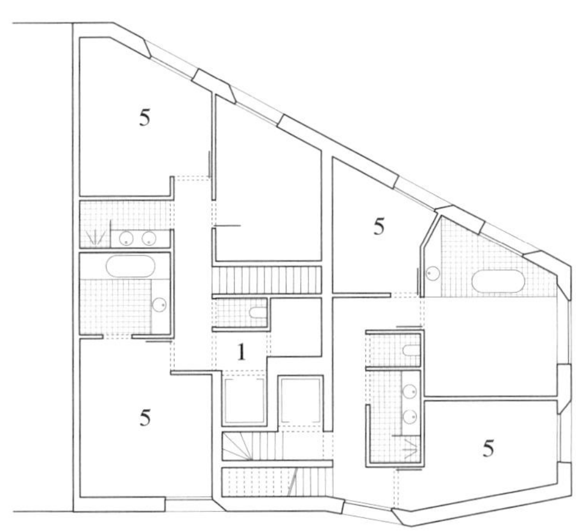

Floor 3

1 entrance
2 terrace
3 living room
4 dining room
5 bedroom
6 patio

BRANDWEG

KAMERS
LIFT
TRAPPEN
WC
MEETING 1 & 2
INTERNET
BAR : LOUNGE
RESTO

Next to the existing youth hostel that was housed in an old school building, there is, on the site on the Passionistenlaan in Kortrijk, a Lourdes grotto and a neo-Romanesque red-brick church. The plot is surrounded by a brick wall with brick arches.

URA extended the existing brick street wall and gave it a clear end by placing a new wall in red concrete perpendicularly to it. The wall and its extension thus encompass all the buildings on the site. The architects, who also drew up the master plan, moved the hostel from a concealed place in the middle of the plot to a remote corner visible from the railway. The building was rotated by a quarter turn with regard to the Passionistenlaan, where the building's main entrance is located. The new hostel hovers over the street wall with a single rib.

The concrete cube, a monolith of prefab concrete whose colours blend in with those of the surrounding brick buildings, comprises a mix of guest rooms. There is room for 123 beds, distributed over 38 rooms (each accommodating between 2 and 6 people). They are arranged around a compact core with a functional spiral staircase. The rooms have been given a rather rough finish, but the window frames have been designed meticulously. Each floor offers a view over the city, each time from another façade or surface of the cube.

The ground floor comprises two multipurpose rooms, a bar and a counter (which are connected to one another), a restaurant with a self-service area, a fully equipped institutional kitchen and a self-catering kitchen. The interiors are separated from each other by a system of wings of concrete discs, a system which also serves as the building's structural frame. The formal idiom is pursued in the built-in furniture. This public plinth is furthermore completely glazed, with the exception of the shaft with staircase leading to the caretaker's apartment that is part of the monolith. Between the transparent plinth and the existing enclosing wall, outdoor rooms emerge, intermediate spaces in the sequence from outside to inside. [ed]

Floor 0

1 entrance
2 courtyard
3 back office
4 meeting room
5 bar
6 refectory
7 self-service
8 kitchen
9 staff room
10 entrance concierge

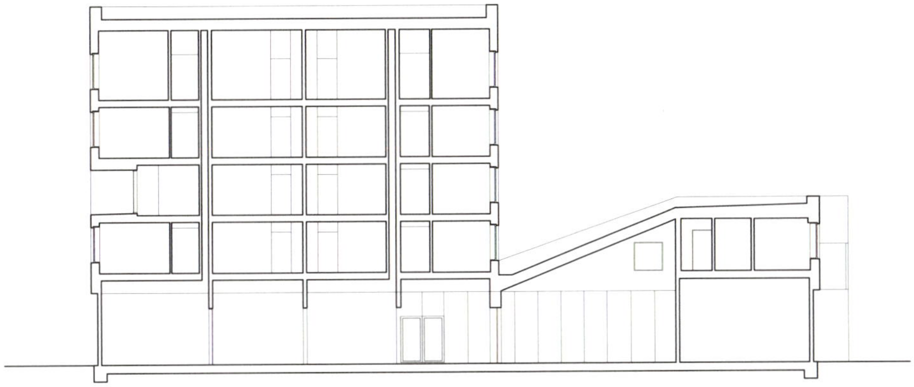

Section Aa

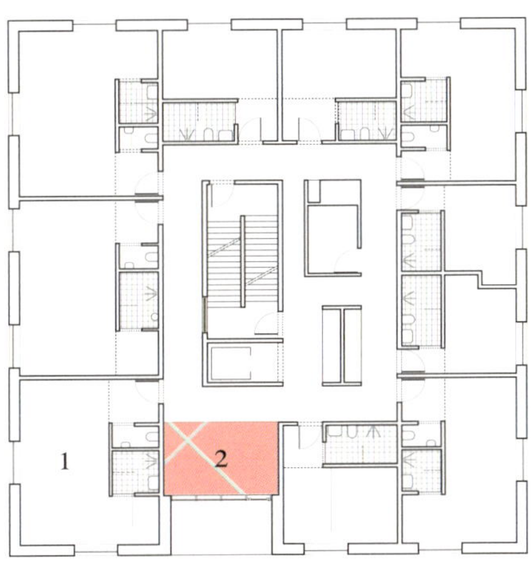

Floor 2

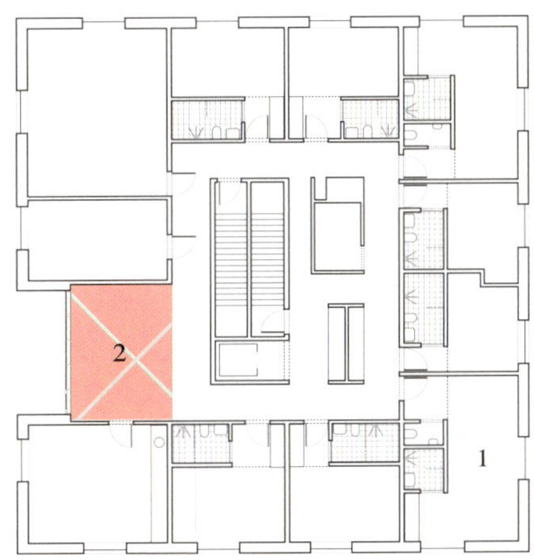

Floor 4

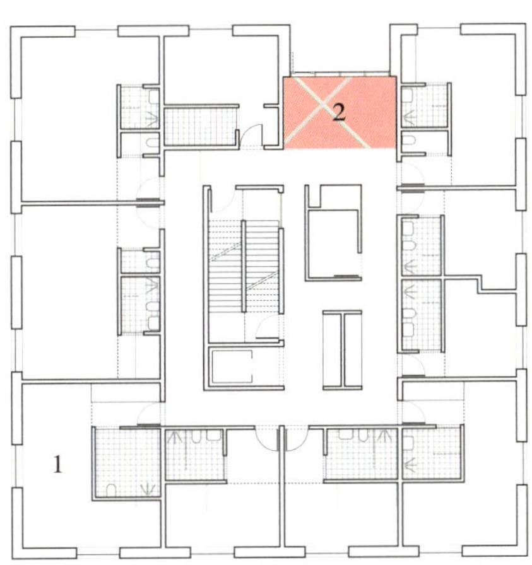

Floor 1

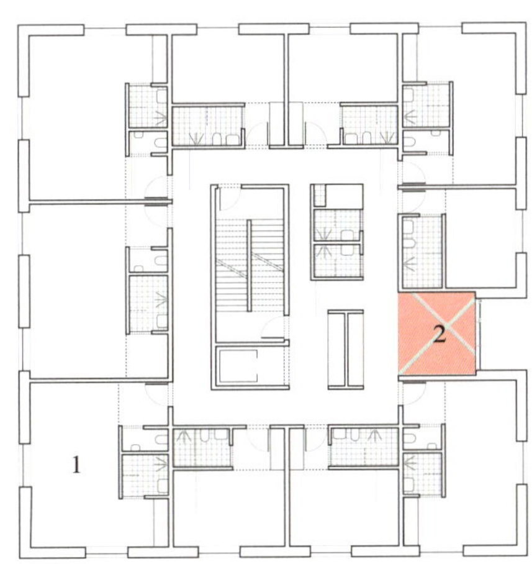

Floor 3

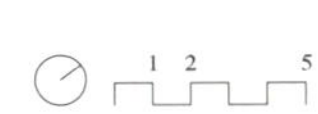

1 room
2 vista

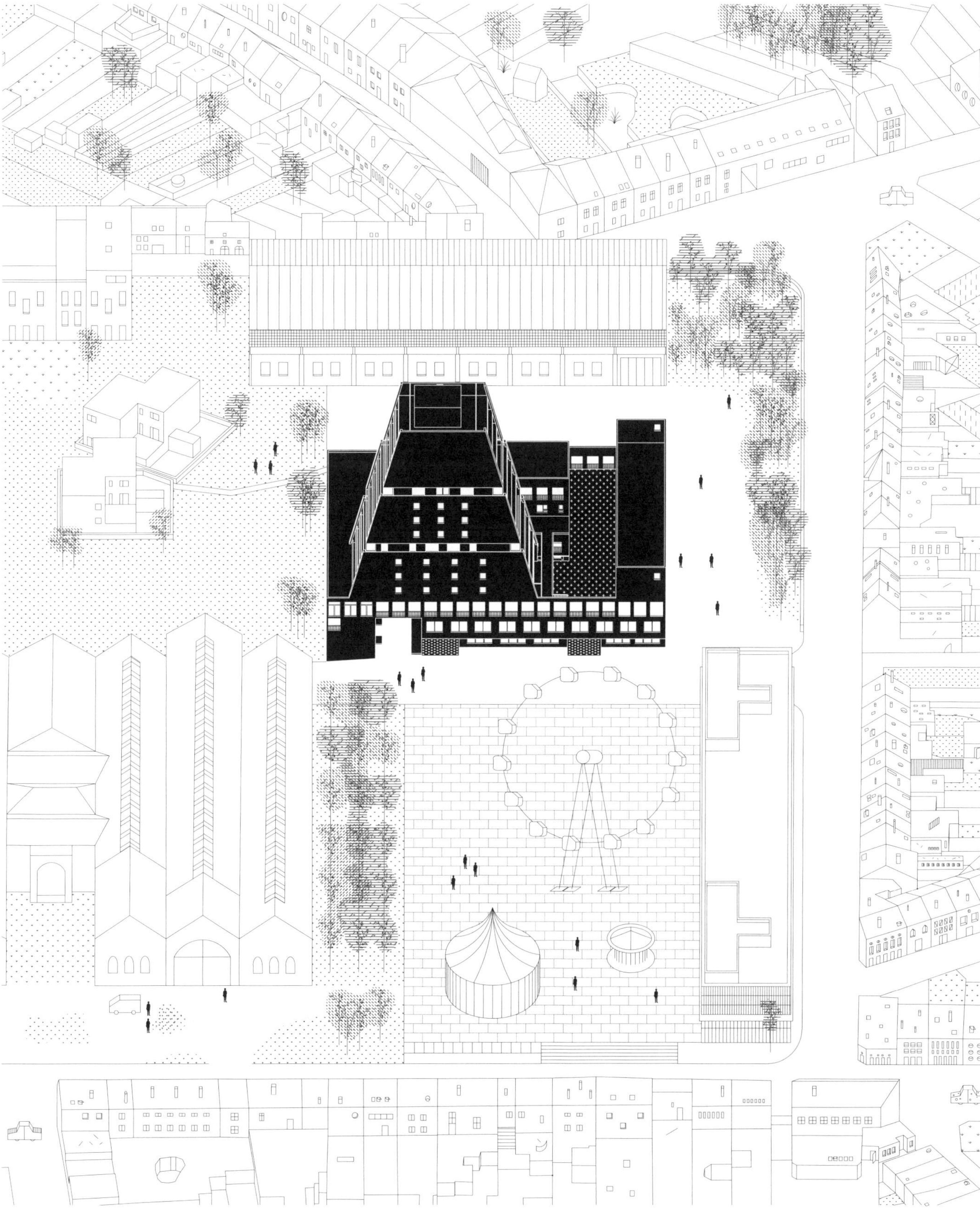

WWL or the Wisselspoor is a complex consisting of 52 family dwellings combined with a series of collective functions, a crèche, a *grand café* and a conservatoire. The project came about thanks to a competition organized by the Autonoom Gemeentebedrijf of the City of Leuven, commissioner and owner of the plot.

The plot is the last unbuilt parcel of the Centrale Werkplaatsen, an 8.5 ha former railway workshop in Kessel-Lo, behind the Leuven train station. At the end of the last century, urban planner Marcel Smets drew up the master plan for the new development of this plot: it provided for the conversion of the existing sheds, the construction of new dwellings, a park, and two squares.

The commissioner wanted to use this last plot to provide an answer to the dual challenge facing this new district: to bring more life into the area and to offer an alternative to private urban developments which, owing to increased pressure on the housing market, are proving to be unaffordable for families and young people.

URA designed ten different housing types, including park villas, bungalows, terraced houses and greenhouse houses. They are distributed over the entire volume and are connected by a public footpath that starts on Blauwputplein and runs to the top of the tower via sloping surfaces, terraces, squares and stairs. Each dwelling has its front door – and therefore its address – on the interior street in this three-dimensional neighbourhood.

Collective functions alternate every four floors with the dwellings, and therefore divide the large volume up in order to bring it back to a human scale. Both the dwellings in the tower and those in the base have a community centre with café and a multipurpose hall or library. There are also shared workshops, bicycle storage facilities and collective outdoor spaces. The crèche, the café and the conservatoire ensure a lively base that provides the Wisselspoor with four front façades: one for each square or park which the project overlooks. [ldv]

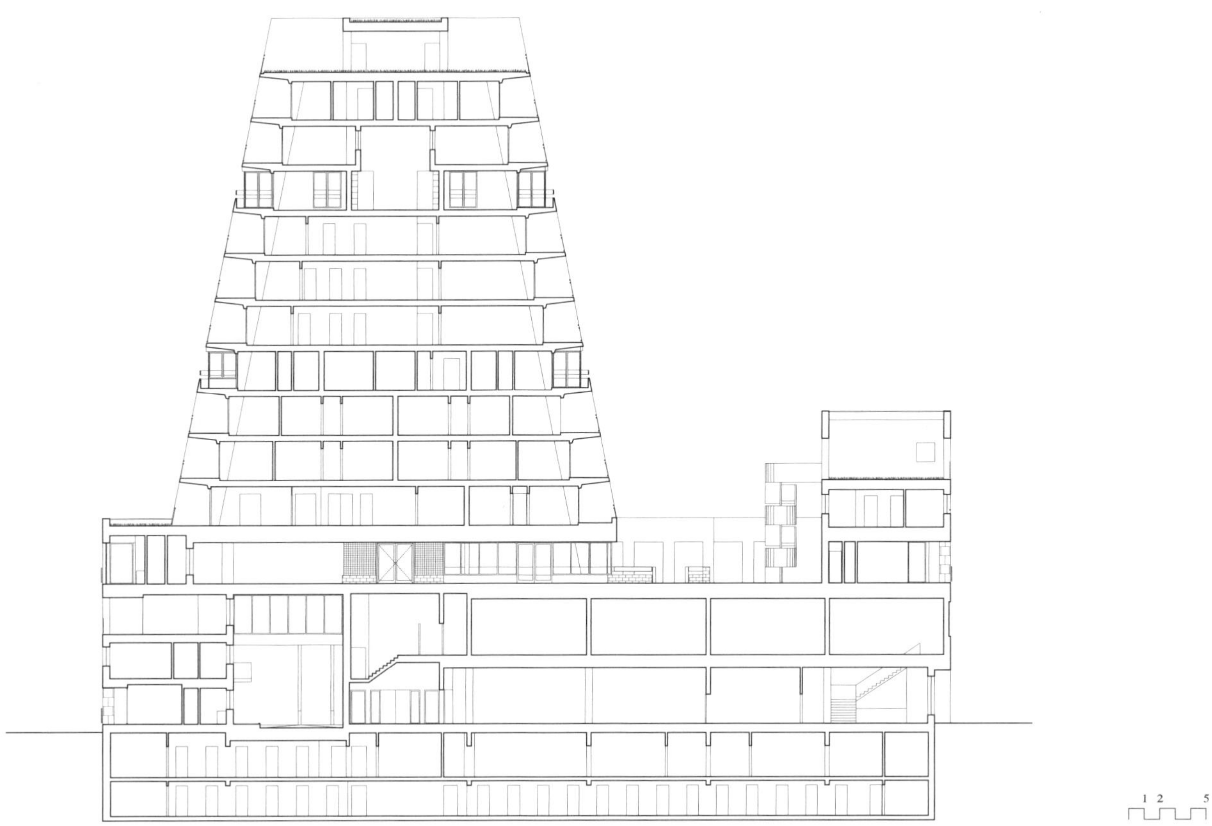

Section Aa

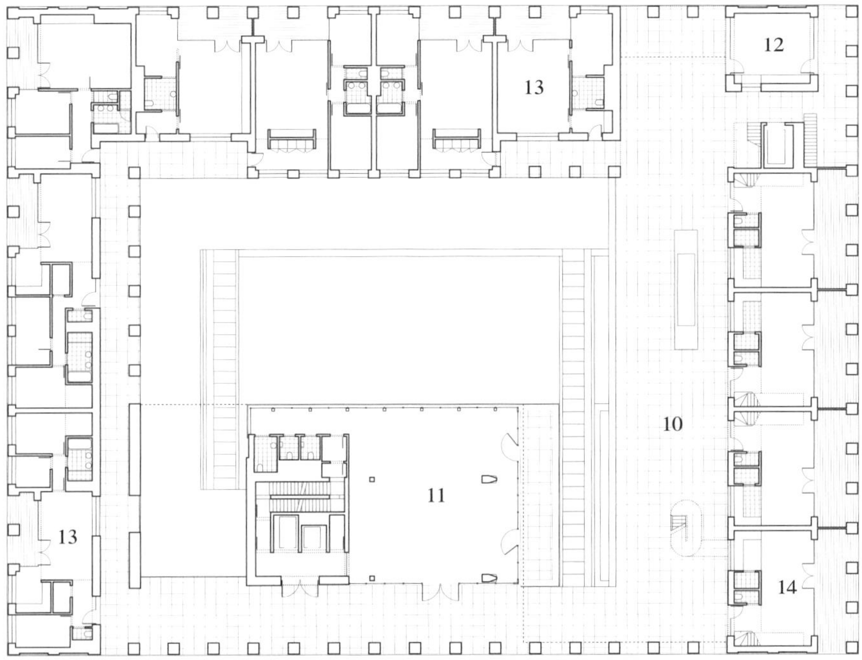

Floor 3

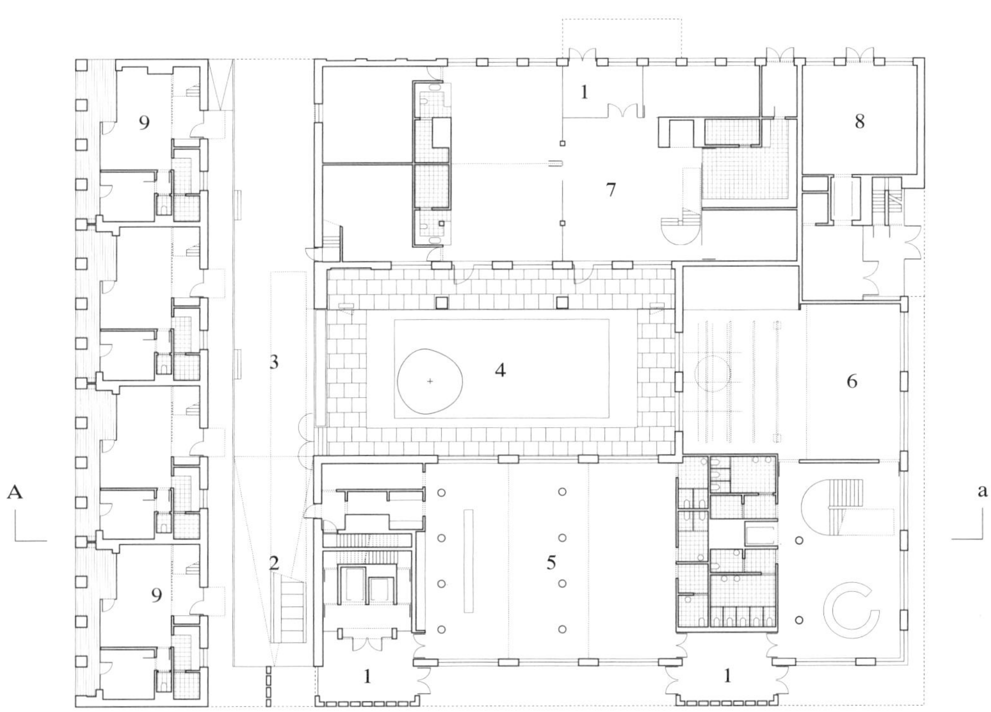

Floor 0

1 entrance
2 ramp
3 passageway
4 courtyard garden
5 grand café
6 conservatory
7 crèche
8 bicycle storage
9 park house
10 collective terrace
11 community centre
12 home office
13 bungalow
14 urban villa

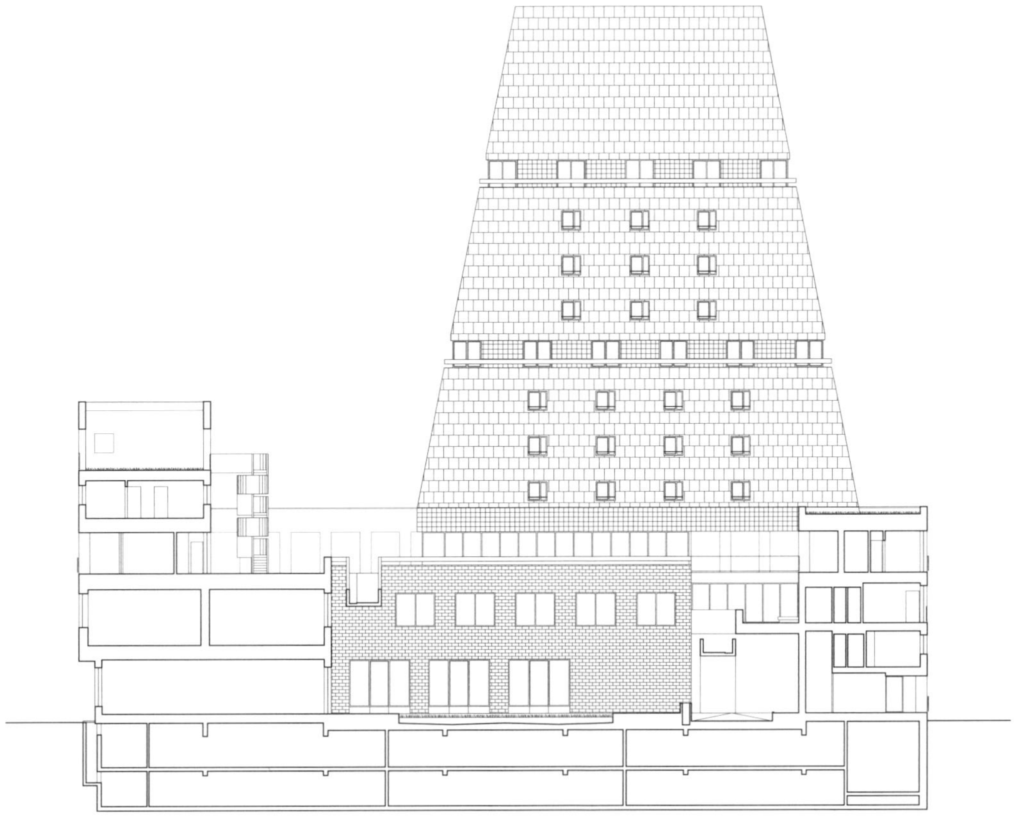

Section Bb

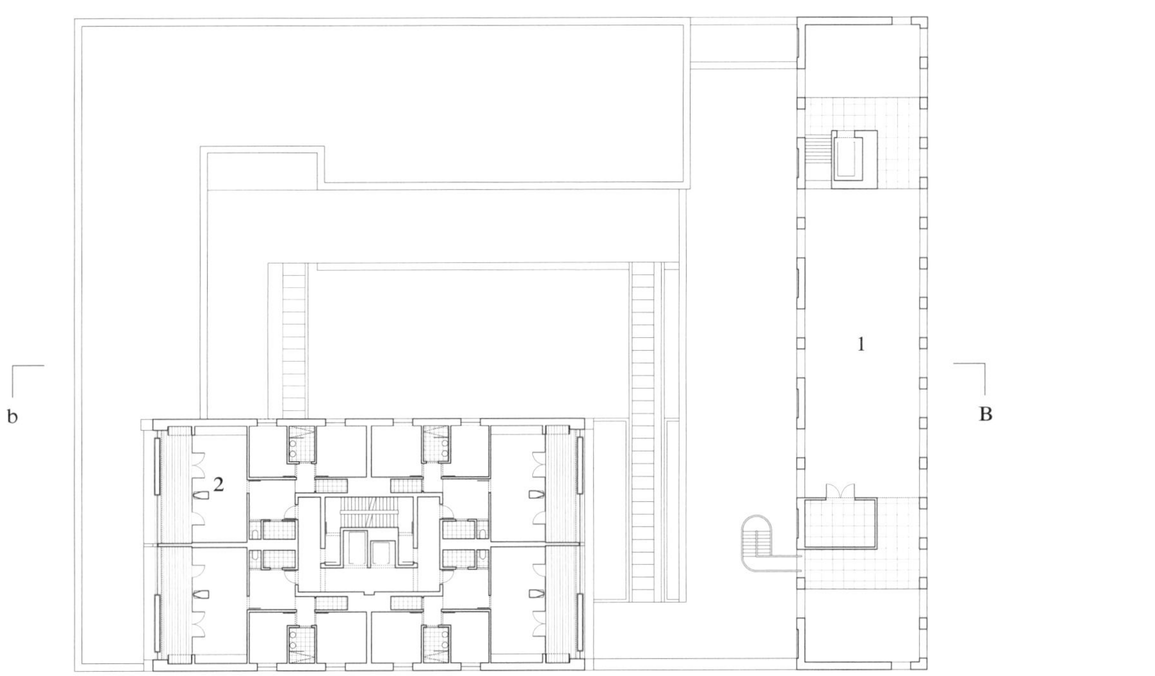

Floor 5

1 roof garden
2 corner house

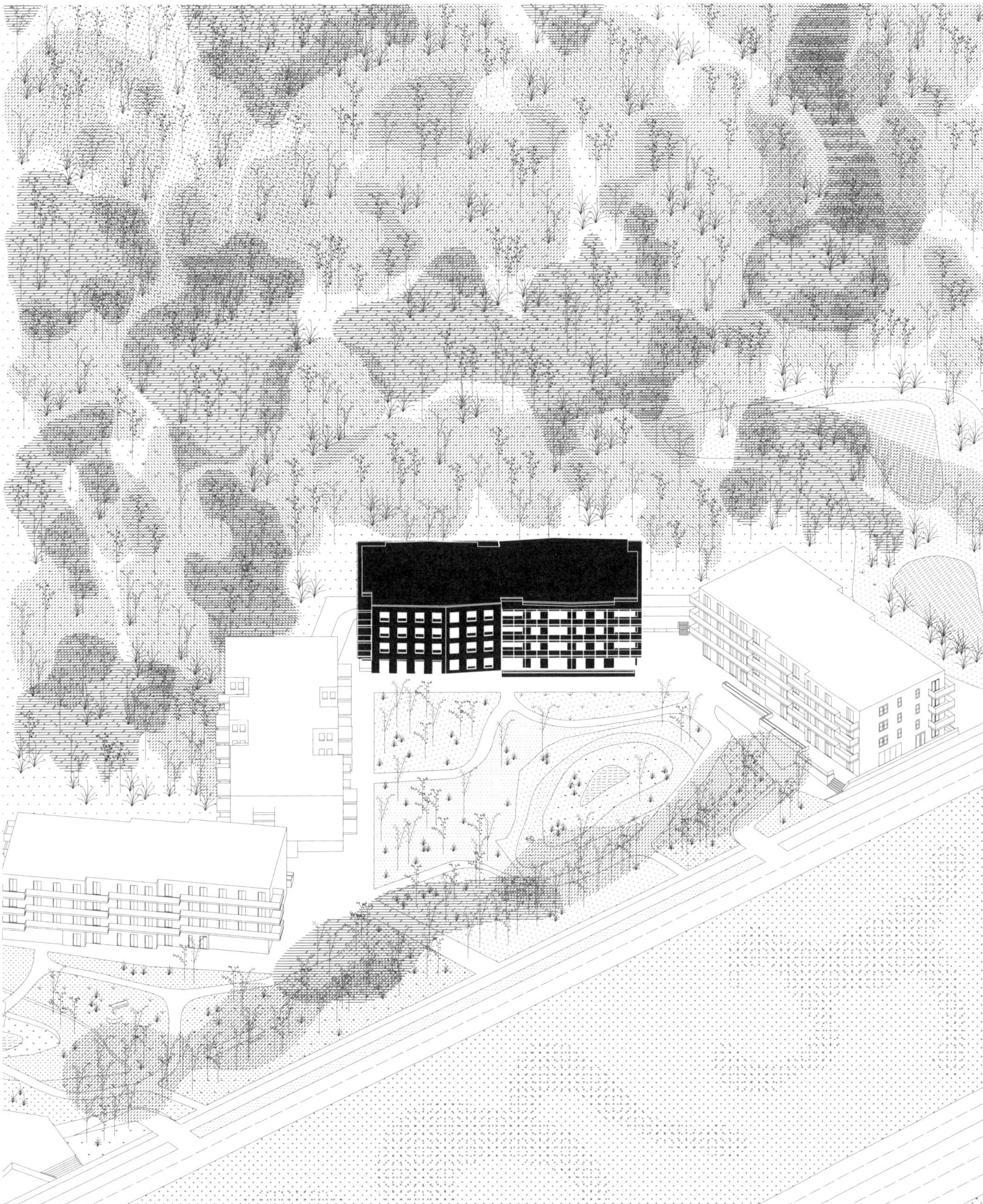

In 2019 Ghent's city development agency SOGENT organized a competition for 52 apartments on a woody plot on the bank of the river Leie. URA won this competition in collaboration with ECTV (Els Claessens and Tanja Vandenbussche) and DVVT (De Vylder Vinck Taillieu architecten) and the project developer 3D. The plot lies hidden behind an industrial site and a small residential area but is in fact ideally located thanks to its proximity to the Gent-Sint-Pieters train station, the ring road and the access to the E40 motorway.

The architects designed six four-storey buildings on a concrete base that follows the irregular border of the wood and thus forms the transition between the wood and the park. This concrete surface constitutes the residents' site of interaction and meeting. It is only accessible to pedestrians since cyclists and car drivers park underground, and it gives access, via small squares between the buildings, to the apartments and the collective and commercial spaces on the ground floor. Each architectural office was in charge of two buildings and developed different housing typologies for this purpose. DVVT designed a series of apartments open from front to back and connected to three circulation cores. ECTV arranged gallery apartments around a communal courtyard. URA, by contrast, combined corner apartments with apartments open from front to back around two circulation cores and constricted by two elongated terraces on the diagonally opposite corners. In total, this has produced about 20 different housing types and therefore a broad choice for the potential buyers. The coherence of the whole is preserved thanks to clear agreements in terms of composition and the palette of materials used in the façades.

By having the concrete base at the front connect directly with the ground level and by designing spaces for commercial services such as shops, the architects managed not to turn this ensemble into an island, but to establish a connection with the dwellings and offices in the area.

A seventh building with social housing will complete the project in the future. [ldv]

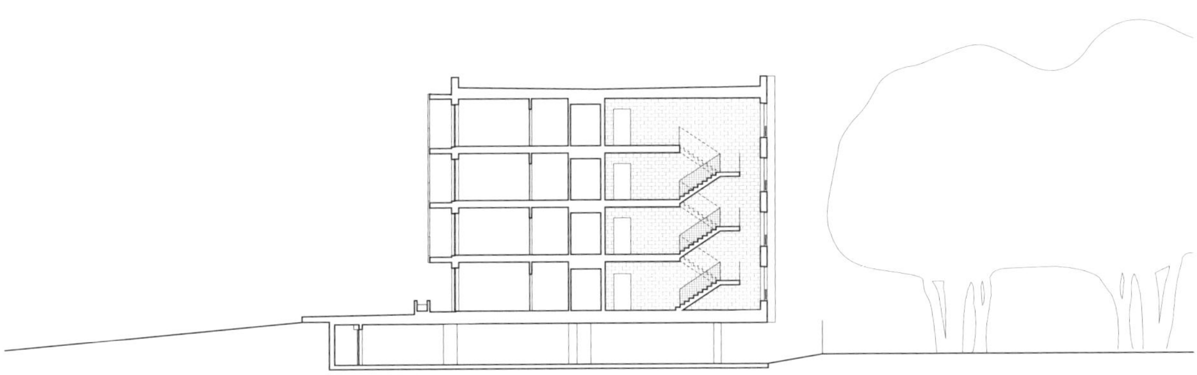

I

II

Section Aa

I Park
II Forest

Section Bb

Floor 1

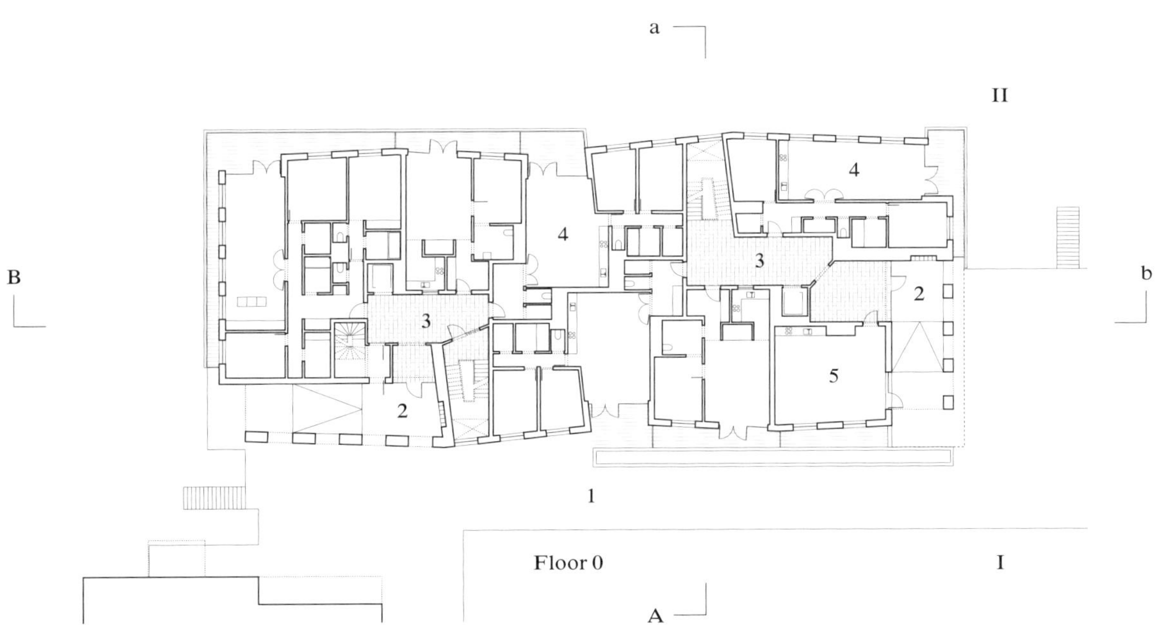

Floor 0

I Park
II Forest

1 deck
2 entrance
3 hall
4 apartment
5 collective space

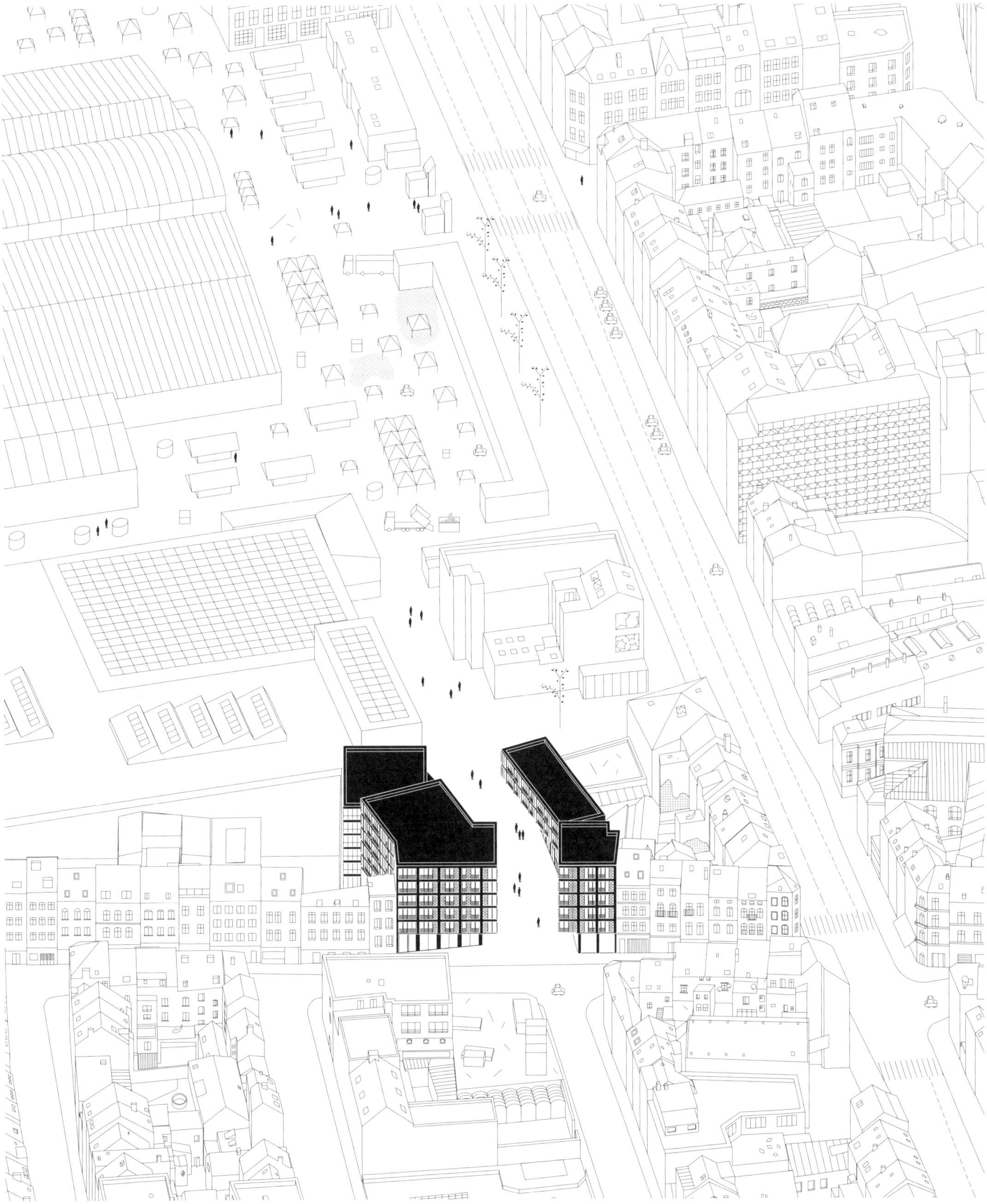

Located in the municipality of Anderlecht, the Abattoir district is undergoing a radical transformation. The introduction of housing into this area is one of the many projects of territorial interest represented by the redevelopment of the Canal that traverses the Brussels metropolis. The project is a genuine fringe area in the urban fabric that is still lacking in social and housing mixity.

The Brussels-South train station with its important weekly market and the Abattoir are landmarks that form a 'chain', as it were, of market activities. The area is an appropriate place in which to include housing on the site and in doing so to consolidate community life in a rapidly changing context.

The project rests on the creation of two large volumes, arranged on either side of the site's central axis, perpendicular to the historical course of the river Senne. Each of these volumes forms a base on which stand two buildings devoted to student housing and family apartments (ranging from studios to three-bedroom units). The design raises the height of the dwellings, giving them unobstructed views and setting them back somewhat from the urban bustle, while also providing an extensive covered public space.

Common areas resembling real hanging squares are to be found here and there among the upper storeys, inside what constitutes a link between two buildings on the same base. Residents can meet in these areas and take part in joint activities in comfortable spaces. On the ground, the complex as a whole constitutes the southern 'gateway' to the site, whose exterior layout makes up another extension of the public space.

The underlying idea seems to be the creation of a sense of community, both in terms of the apartment buildings and the neighbourhood. Sequences of built spaces (both private and shared) as well as areas reserved for strolling and other more informal activities also help to establish a new neighbourhood life. And it is perhaps here that can be found the possibility of a unification of the urban landscape, on the scale of encounters. [fcn]

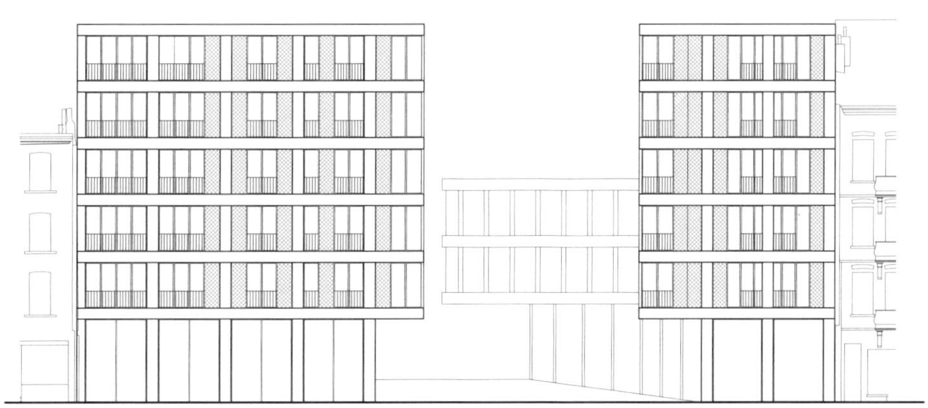

South elevation

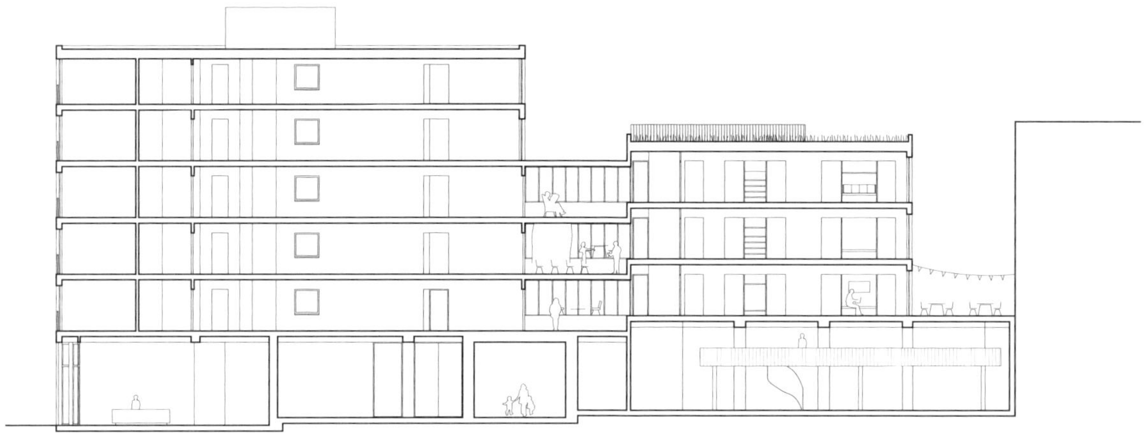

Section Aa

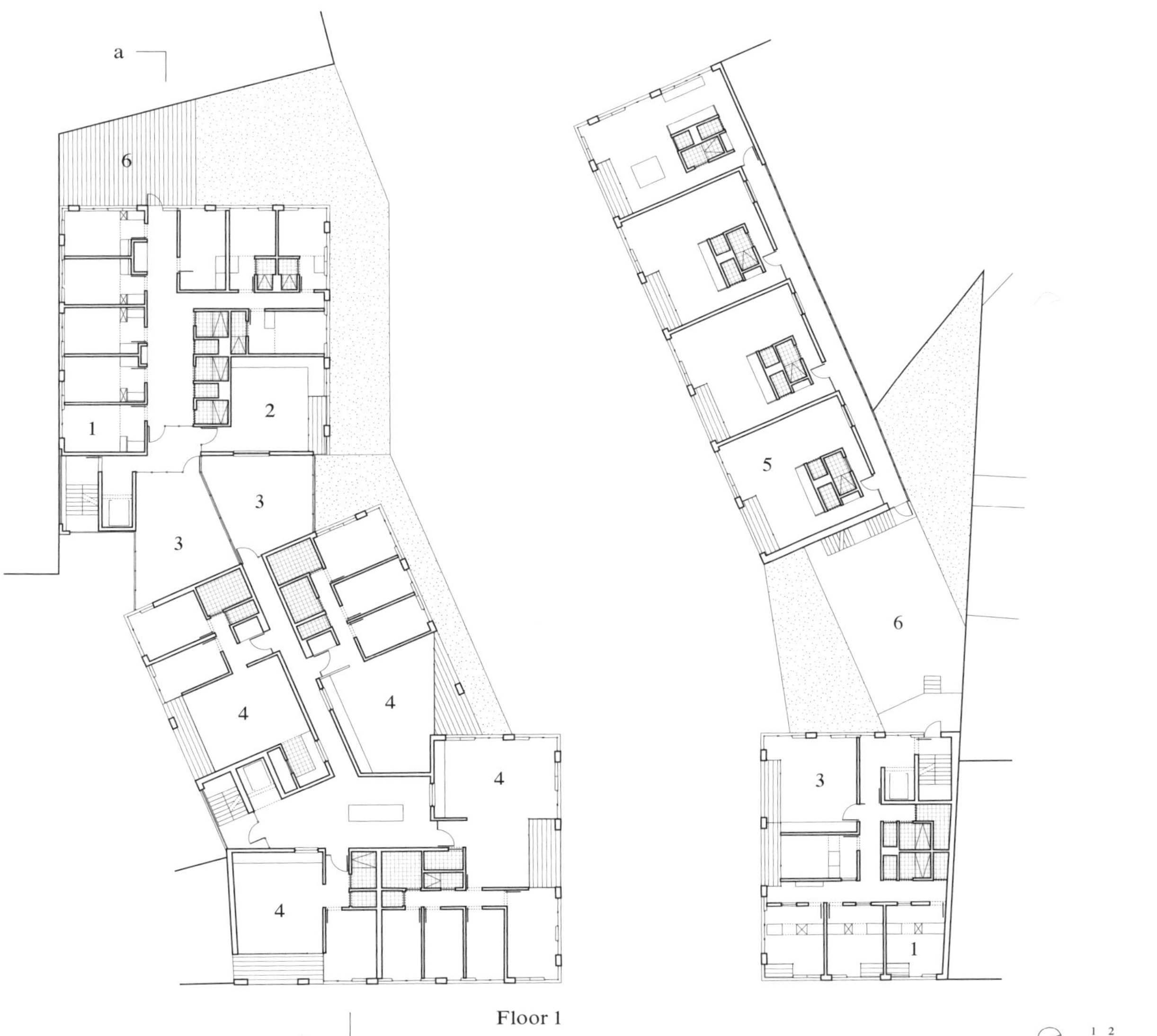

Floor 1

1 student room
2 kitchen
3 collective space
4 house
5 studio
6 collective roof terrace

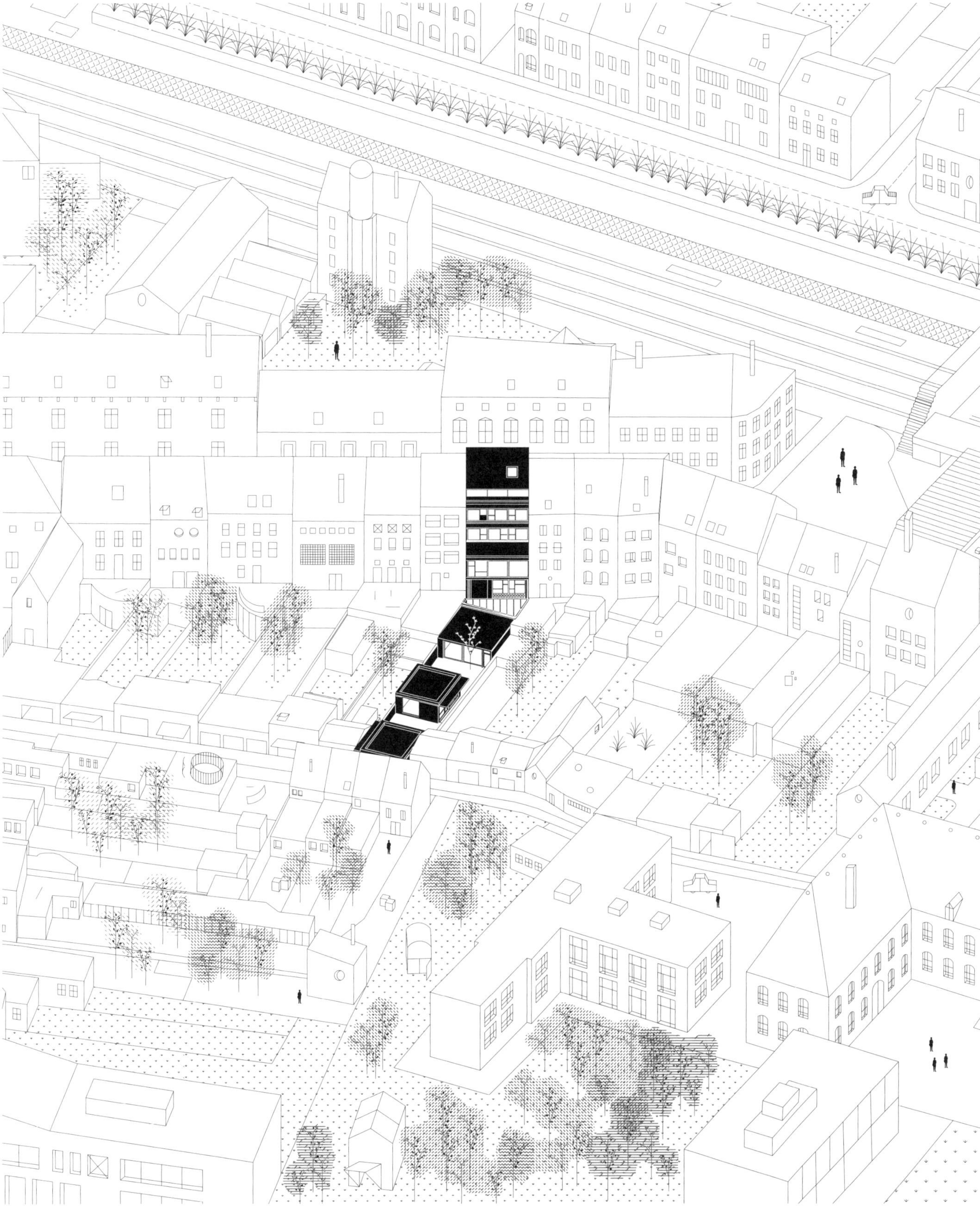

'Locomotief', a rehabilitation centre for children, is the result of a radical conversion of a town house commissioned by the health-insurance fund Christelijke Mutualiteiten.

The stately front façade gives onto a classical street that was laid in the late nineteenth century and that connects the rehabilitation centre with the train station. At the back, the long plot gives onto a narrow alley with small workers' houses. The architects responded to this break in scale with a project comprising several volumes and therefore fitting into the streetscape on both sides, giving access from both streets.

The original house was in such a poor state that it was demolished. Only the front façade was preserved and restored. As the sole remnant of the town house, it now functions as a piece of scenery, as it were, behind which the wings are hidden. These take the shape of a series of interior walls set perpendicularly to the plot boundaries that separate the successive indoor and outdoor rooms from each other. The ground floor consists of a long sequence that runs from the front façade through the main building and the first patio, via the exercise room through the second patio and along the medical practice at the back before coming back out onto the street. Light and perspectives also traverse the building.

To heighten the independent status of the front wall, the architects placed a monumental open staircase between the façade and the main volume. This staircase not only serves as a dividing void, but also forms an important vertical meeting place for the parents and children of the centre. That's why the architects designed a bench on each floor where parents can wait while their children are in rehab.

The rear façade of the main volume consists of three descending terraces. Thanks to the bend in the plot, they offer views over the area and the green hills around Ninove. The terraces also form the second escape route. [ldv]

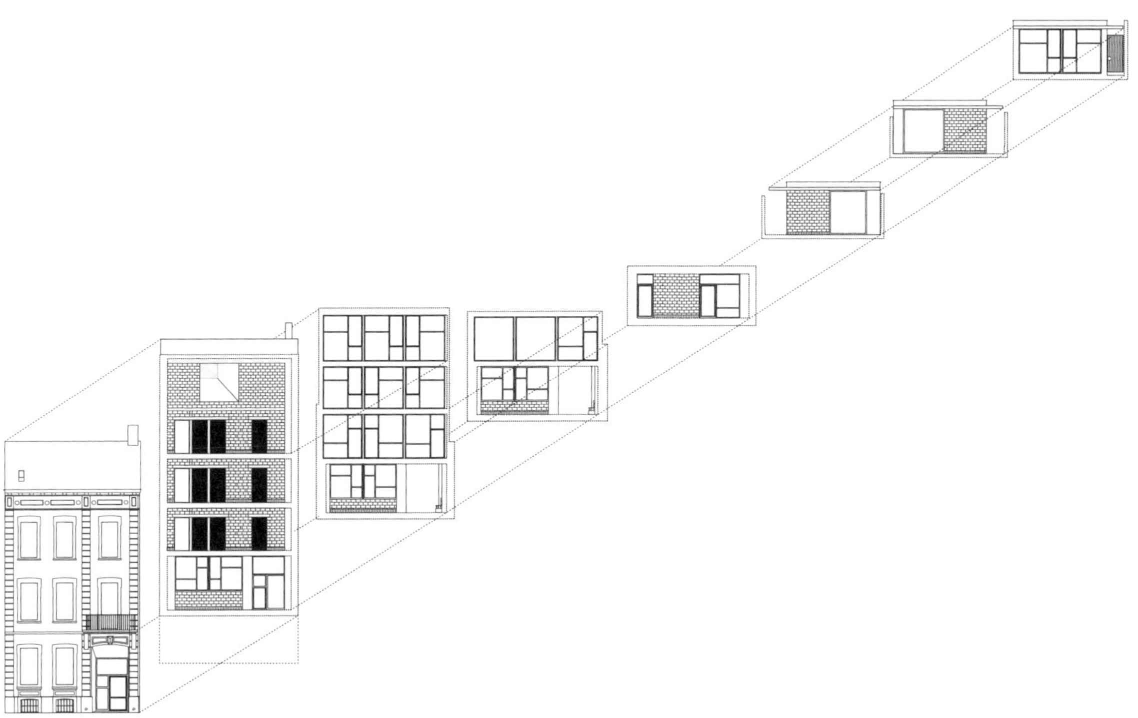

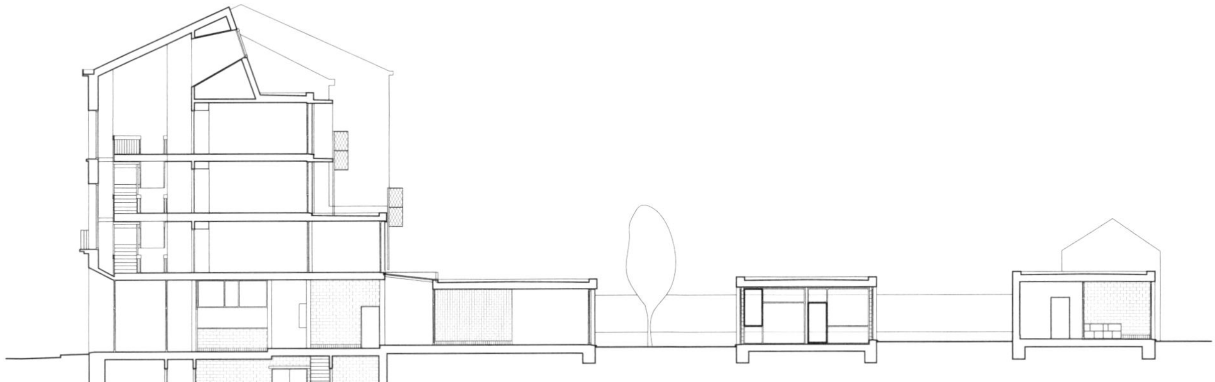

Section Aa

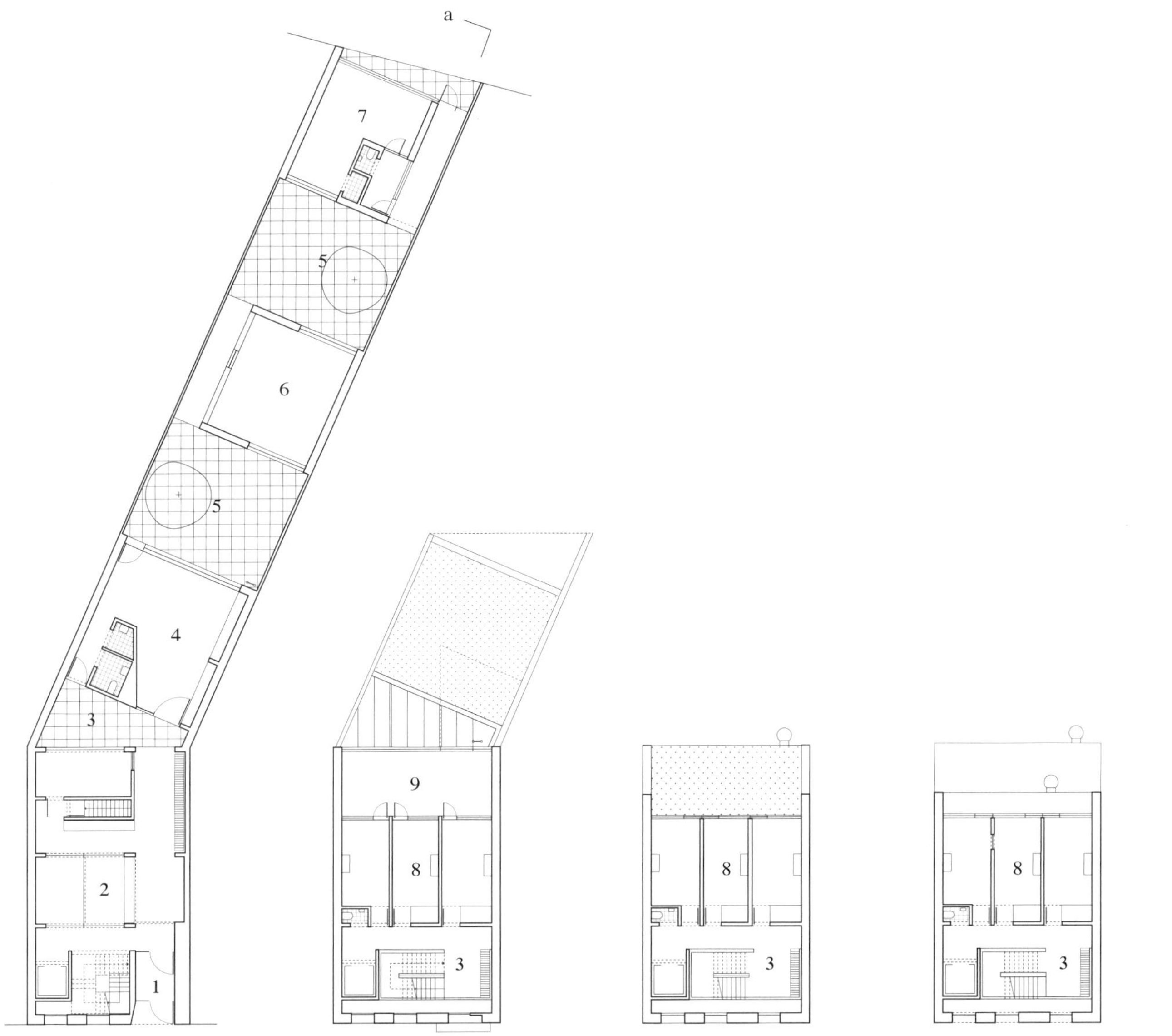

Floor 0 Floor 1 Floor 2 Floor 3

1 entrance
2 reception
3 waiting area
4 meeting room
5 patio
6 physiotherapy
7 medical cabinet
8 therapy
9 group therapy

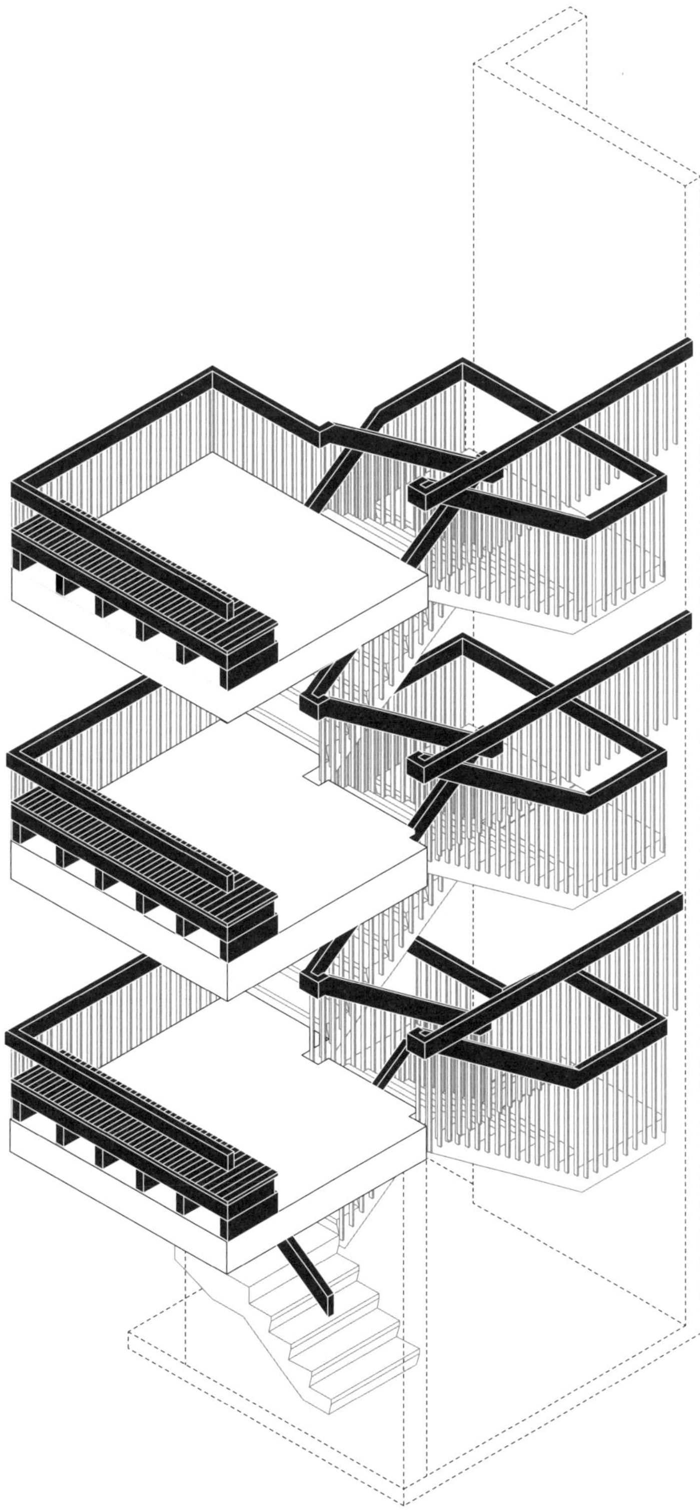

WZK

Residential care centre

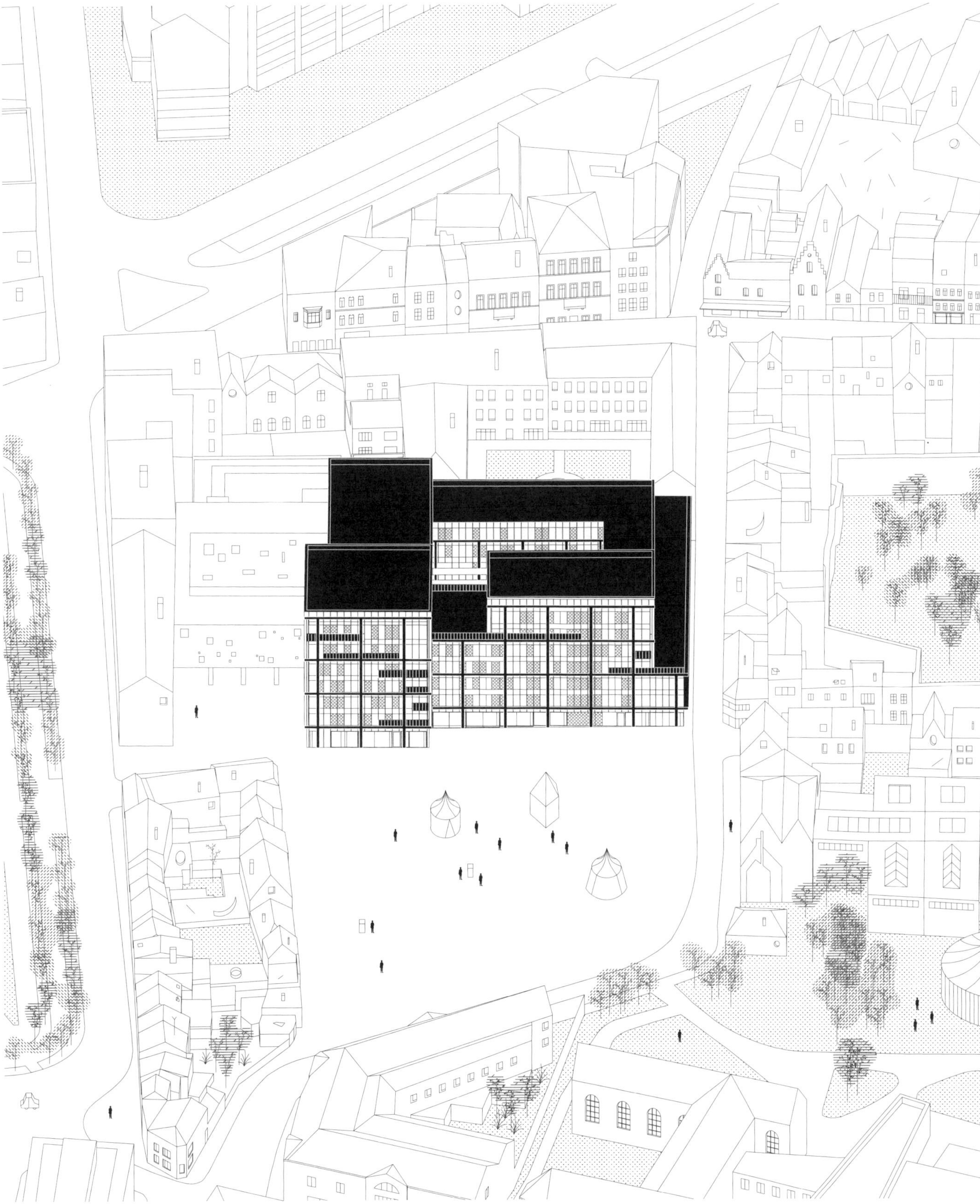

Kortrijk

When the hospital beside the Sint-Niklaas monastery in the centre of Kortrijk moved into new quarters outside the city, the building was razed and space was made for the construction of an assisted-living centre commissioned by GVO.

The architects pursued the monastery typology and designed a complex built around two patios and overlooking the monastery garden and another existing courtyard. One of the new patios is fully open to the public space and thus makes the connection to a series of connected squares and parks bordering the plot.

The main building comprises five storeys and thus ties in, in terms of volume, to the adjacent fabric. Two extra storeys were added to the central wing and the two corners overlooking the square – storeys that, like little towers, offer views of and for the city. The massiveness of the ensemble is broken by the deliberate layered nature of the façade. A corset-like concrete grid embraces the building and introduces a first rhythm. Horizontal strips and raised ribs in brass emphasize the storeys and the vertical window division in a second rhythm, finished by black metal parapets. This layered quality not only lends depth and variation to what is potentially, given the programme, a monotonous façade composition, but transforms the assisted-living centre into a building that helps determine the view of the city.

Inside, the concrete column structure has been left visible and serves to organize the space. The glazed plinth forms a link between the reception, collective spaces and the patios. It is therefore an important meeting place for both residents and visitors.

On the upper floors, the architects designed compact rooms that alternate with storage closets that made it possible to do away with storage spaces in favour of large collective living areas and terraces overlooking the city. The other pieces of furniture – from the benches in the lobby and the café to the bedrooms and living rooms – were also designed by the architects. [ldv]

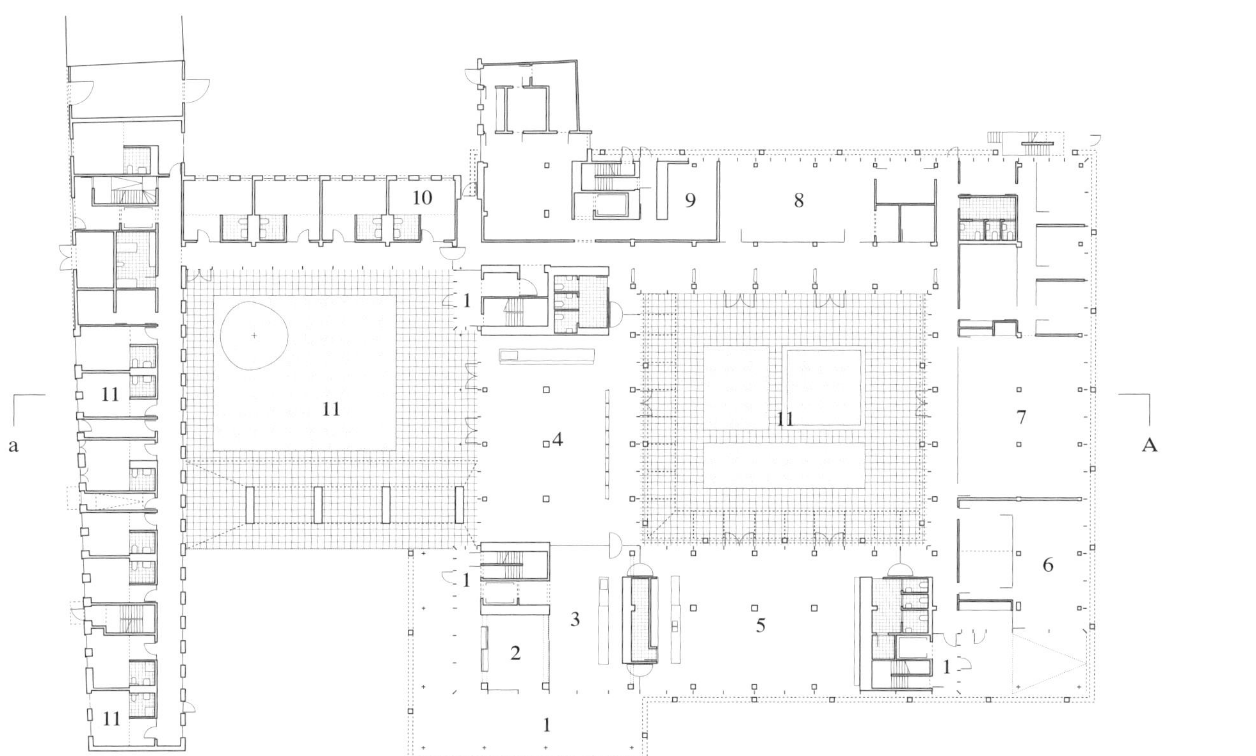

Floor 0

1 entrance
2 lobby
3 reception
4 restaurant
5 grand café
6 auditorium
7 administration
8 wellness
9 hairdresser
10 room
11 courtyard

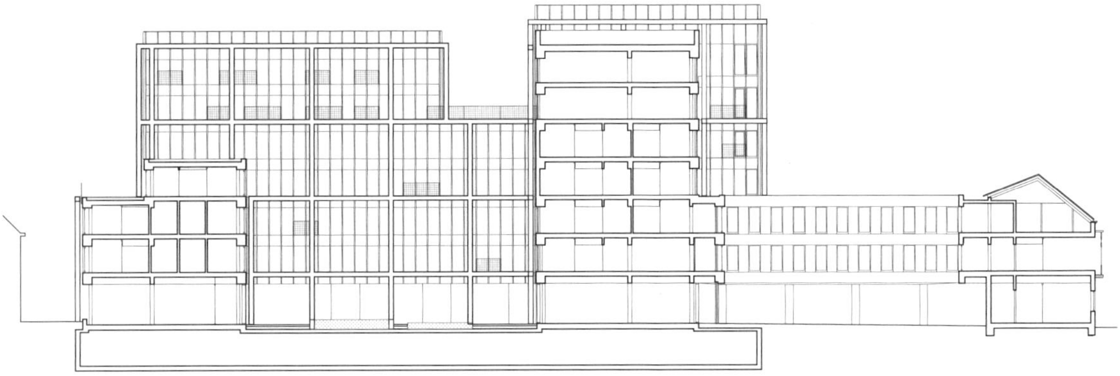

Section Aa

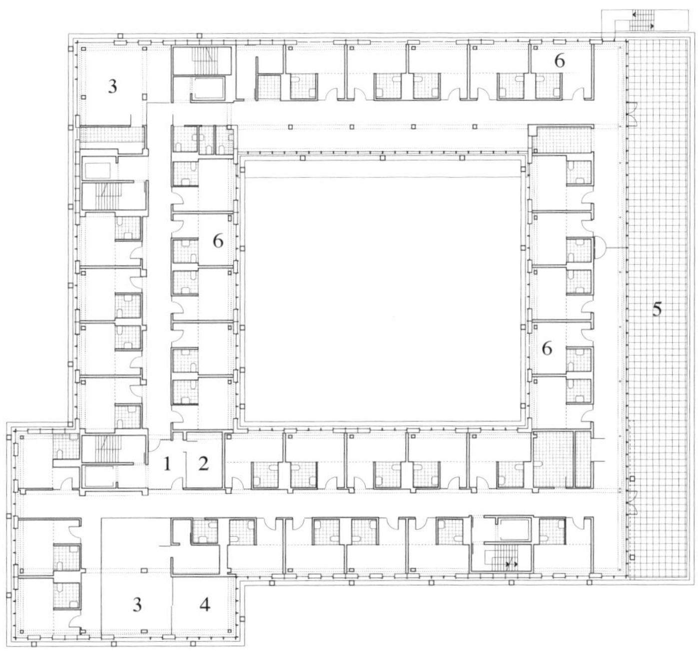

Floor 3

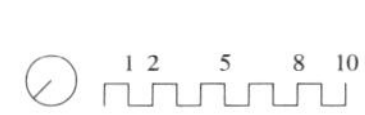

1 entrance
2 nursing station
3 dining area
4 winter garden
5 balcony
6 room

ITW

Lisa De Visscher and Iwan Strauven
in conversation with Yves Malysse and Kiki Verbeeck

At your request, this interview is taking place in Le Parador, a villa in the Brussels region that Belgian architect Jacques Dupuis built in 1948 and extended in 1954. Why is this house so important to you?

The work of Jacques Dupuis has a special meaning for us. In 2002, when the office had just been founded, the first monograph on Dupuis was published. At the time we were working on two projects with a very specific housing programme – the FAR house in Roeselare and a loft in Antwerp – and as young, hungry architects, we were looking for different insights in all sorts of ways. To be honest, we didn't know Dupuis's work well at the time, but when we got our hands on the book and saw the project for Le Parador, suddenly a lot of the pieces of the puzzle fell into place. This house has a very dense programme in which all the pleasures of living can come to the fore. There are several reception rooms, lounges and a majestic dining area, each of which engages in a separate relationship with the large garden. What is unique about this house is how living is staged in all these spaces. Dupuis uses a very specific and rich vocabulary in which materiality, formal language and staging play a key role. He succeeds in designing the interiors in such a way that each space is given a specific atmosphere that contrasts with the preceding space and the following one. To achieve this, he employs highly classical elements which, in terms of materiality for example, are then implemented in a very unusual manner. You also notice that the house is a turning point in Dupuis' oeuvre. On the one hand you can feel the traditional roots that feed the design of the house, while on the other hand, modernism is breaking through at different places. You feel, as it were, the stubborn belief in the freedom of architecture and the fact that, as an architect, you can leave your own stamp on the various places within the house. That lends the whole a certain depth, and the house becomes a story with several layers. Through his specific use of materials and striking interiors, Dupuis created an area of tension that impressed us at the time and that has continued to influence our work to this day.

This house is a *Gesamtkunstwerk*. How does this fit in with your way of working?

Just like Jacques Dupuis, we like to go far in the design of all the (hidden) layers of the programme. For us, the dissection of the programme is an essential starting point of the design process. We deliberately use 'programme' and not 'functions'. An assignment is often reduced to a list of the various functions the building must contain, but life, and more specifically housing, is so much more. When analysing the programme, we think in terms of scenarios: what happens on a typical weekday or at the weekend? Where do everyday actions such as cooking or washing take place? And what about mental activities like reading and thinking while drinking a coffee or a whiskey? We start out from these physical, mental and emotional actions and events to shape the design. Architecture is for us the decor in which daily rituals are given a place. So we sometimes almost literally stage the scenarios, create certain atmospheres, without for that matter dictating actions or controlling users all too consciously. That's why we like to work so much with what we call 'disrupters'. Elements that bring about friction in the space and so offer multiple possibilities of use. Here too there is an area of tension that is in line with what Jacques Dupuis has made here.

> Dupuis is a stubborn architect in modernism, in part because he incorporates atypical typologies and archetypes into his architecture such as the tower in this house. This lends depth and complexity to his version of modernism. Does this fascinate you too?

Modernism is a style. We don't want to concern ourselves with styles, however. Dupuis is indeed more interesting than the textbook modernist who builds very austere architecture, because many styles and elements from different periods come together here and the design and construction are therefore less dogmatic. We, too, want to draw a broad picture, to weave history into architecture in an abstract and not a literal way, and in doing so to unite different things into one.

> The name of your office refers to Ur, the first city. In your work, you talk about creating an archetype that is confronted with the context. How does this happen exactly?

We talked previously about the way we make the programme our own and convert it to space. Parallel to this, another process unfolds, namely how we develop a volumetry from the archetype and fit it into the context. This spatial context is very important to us. Its analysis is very intuitive. Sometimes we literally drive around a place for a few days in a Volkswagen van and even camp there to really get to know the site. The building we add to the environment must be an added value and must be able to stand the test of time. There can be some resistance, some friction between the building and its surroundings. But we do want to accompany the user to the building, we want to guide the entry. The volume emerges from these analyses and considerations, unambiguously and concisely. After which we confront this volume with the programme, and one can explain – or contradict – the other. Both are interesting. It is a very fruitful moment because you can then choose to focus on one or the other and so steer the design process. This always happens on the border between the rational and the emotional, the pragmatic and the intuitive, the functional or structural and the gut feeling.

> Do you consciously look for monumentality in your work? Is the sculptural element in your oeuvre an expression of this?

Monumentality is certainly not a goal in itself for us. Neither is the sculptural element, but it does play a major role in our work. Over the years we have gained a lot of confidence in the plasticity

of architecture. By designing and building, we have learned how to wring and fold a building into what we had in mind. The search for abstraction and monumentality is a search for the recognizable. We develop forms derived from familiar forms from history so that a new form arises that still carries that recognizable element within it. A good example is WWL in Leuven. The ziggurat-shaped tower refers to a historical archetype, but it was sculpted so carefully that not only does the programme fit in it perfectly, but the courtyard also gets enough light and the square around it now has an anchor. We never use a form for the sake of the form. That would be a matter of formalism and that doesn't interest us.

WWL, p. 146

The youth hostel in Kortrijk also grew out of a sculpted form and the ambition to create a distinguishing landmark in the city. In both projects, the result possesses a certain lack of scale and therefore monumentality. However, the reason for this was the search for identity, and not for monumentality.

In short, over the years we have synchronously developed two ways of working. On the one hand, there is an intuitive way of looking at how a building can nestle in its context. On the other hand, there is a very pragmatic and analytical way of working with the programme, such as the development of an organigram to establish connections between different elements of the programme so that they can be staged in a number of atmospheres, spaces and identities.

This creates a continuous weighing-up of the rational and the emotional, of very pragmatic and very intuitive research. The most interesting moment is when these two are brought together in the design process. And then we like to talk about 'dialectical image', where one begins to cross-pollinate the other.

What exactly do you understand by 'dialectical image'?

We borrowed this concept from Walter Benjamin. For us, it refers to a contradiction that comes together in architecture and creates added value. An image in architecture is never static because you move through architecture. So, it's more about a snapshot, a passage, a transition. If we look in this house by Dupuis from here to there, we see a dialectical image because there is such a stark contrast between the atmospheres and identities of the successive spaces. We believe that the force of a project comes from letting each part of the programme be itself and express itself in all its splendour. This applies just as much to two adjoining rooms as it does to the building in relation to its surroundings. Entering through the shell is crucial because it creates a contrast that intensifies the experience.

Is the way you use your materials crucial in this?

Materiality is indeed extremely important to us because the identity and atmosphere of a place come into their own in the use of materials. We should add that about 85 per cent of our projects are public commissions: buildings erected by, for and with society. The economic factor is always a very important parameter in this respect. Budgets for public buildings have to be adhered to very strictly and the distribution of the available resources is therefore fundamental. This additional precondition helps us more and more because it really is a tool in the design process to reduce a building to its essence. Think of KAU, the gymnasium in Uccle. There the materiality stems, on the one hand, from a structural fact. Because the building is situated in the sloping landscape, we had to provide a concrete retaining wall, which also remains visible in the gymnasium. But in order not to lapse into the levelling of a purely functional building, we added a layer via the materiality that underlines the staging of the various sub-programmes. For example, the changing rooms there were made of concrete blocks, with a clear structural use, but the shower rooms are covered with old-rose tiles, which create tension, conflict and a different materiality so that the purely structural is transcended. This is how we create a new image.

How are the different design techniques you mentioned – sculpting a mass in order to arrive at the ideal form, dissecting the programme, staging – expressed in other projects? Are there other methods you work with?

Teatro Olimpico, Vicenza

During our studies, Palladio's Teatro Olimpico was an eye-opener. We realized at the time how, by means of architecture, by creating spaces and establishing perspectives, you can stage activities and consciously steer actions. By creating decors for the scenarios that contain the programme, we can create spaces of course but also introduce certain materials. The children's rehabilitation centre in Ninove is a good example of this. The project definition states clearly the place of the therapists and children. But nobody had thought of the parents, who were completely missing from the programme. And yet they are the users who often have the most questions, fears and uncertainties. That's why we designed places where parents can meet and talk to each other informally. We introduced benches along the central staircase where parents can wait while their children are being treated. A decor is made, and the play unfolds by itself afterwards.

At the youth hostel in Kortrijk, we designed a very specific route that combines all the standard actions involved in checking in or out: registering, picking up your sheets, handing in your dirty sheets, leaving your luggage, etc. This route also ensures that the rest of the programme falls into place.

In WWL too, the route is the backbone of the design. The walk from the street to the dwellings is more than a simple trajectory from A to B; it's the first part of living itself, where you meet (or avoid) your neighbours, where you take a look at the city or take shelter from the rain. This walk became a means for us to stage everyday life and for that, we had a whole vocabulary at our disposal: heights, depths, perspectives, views of the city, walls to hide behind, little squares to come together and ramps for buggies and trolleys. With the dynamic action of coming home or leaving, we tried to bring the whole project together into one whole.

BLB, p. 96

In Bruges, for the bus station, we were given a very static fact: waiting. But this also contains an interesting scenario. After all, waiting means watching, spying, seeing and being seen, but also taking cover, hiding, or being bored. For this we made specifically designed shelters, as an almost literal interpretation of the primitive hut. We designed all the requested elements – bench, information board, bin and canopy – as a single piece of furniture. We believe that precisely designed spaces allow for different actions. We hope that here, too, consciously or unconsciously, the user will seize the opportunity to appropriate the space as he or she sees fit.

> The façades in your projects always have a distinct spatiality in which a certain complexity was clearly sought after. What significance does the façade have for you in a design?

The façade is indeed one of the most direct ways of communicating with the public and the environment. For us, designing a façade means entering into a dialogue with the place, telling the story from the inside and granting a first look at what is hidden behind it.

WZK, p. 174

The assisted-living centre in Kortrijk probably has the most layered façade in our work. This layeredness refers to the complexity of the place in which many different scales and typologies come together: the typology of the old monastery, the density of the programme, the scale of the area and that of the city. We wanted to materialize all these different narratives in the façade. We are very conscious in our use of materials because we want to create a building with a face and a character. The last thing we want is to radiate neutrality. For us it is, again, about creating a sense of identity, both for the building itself and for the place and the neighbourhood.

The research is largely done by means of models of façade fragments on scales ranging from 1:20 to 1:5. This spatial model of the façade is important to us. A façade is not two-dimensional, it is a dynamic action. It's true that we consciously make façades more complex. Today we are overwhelmed by all kinds of standards and rules that make the façade package technically very complex, but most of the time there is nothing to be seen of this on the outside. Because everything has to move fast in the building process, you often get the opposite: a façade that has been completely flattened. We find that a pity. The façade is for us the shell around the decor, the field of tension that forms the boundary between entering and leaving. We want to turn this into a momentum, a place that not only tells the story of inside and out, but also of all the layers in-between.

The use of materials is of course very important, and this is not limited to the façade alone. Specific materials are drawn into the interior and are also part of the justification of certain design choices within the process of architecture that we like to see as a *Gesamtkunstwerk*.

You have succeeded in creating a universe of your own. Not only through your specific design methods and use of materials, but also through the vocabulary you use such as *Tsjoep* (bulge, protrusion), *vleugje* (touch, tinge, spark) and *besnuffelen* (to sniff at). A vocabulary that is far removed from the classical use of words in architecture criticism and that often conjures up very precise images. Is it a deliberate choice to make the language your own within a world in which people think and design in a specific way?

KAU, p. 34

The vocabulary came into being intuitively. We weren't really aware that this is how we were creating our own universe. On the other hand, it is certainly true that we are unconsciously looking for more generic terms for the architectural interventions we make, probably for fear of naming something too unambiguously and thus restricting our work method. Everyone in the office uses these names, including the foreign staff members.

We hardly work with external references to guide or inspire the design process. We have our own language to interpret and translate something plastically, without referring to existing buildings. That doesn't make it any easier in itself. However, we want to keep talking about the design and allow both experimentation and interpretation, and not just copy what already exists. We know very well what we want, but we're not going to link it directly to existing references.

Of course, if we're honest, we already have them in mind. We're all contaminated with images. We have a library, an entire image bank in our heads. But we like to keep those images outside of the office.

What references are we talking about? What specific buildings have influenced you?

Castel Sant'Angelo, Rome

We already mentioned Palladio and Dupuis, but the architecture of Sigurd Lewerentz is also very important to us, and of course Castel Sant'Angelo in Rome. It is a reference that has been with us for years. This stone colossus fascinates us because it possesses so much wealth in terms of both massive materiality and programme diversity. An Italian employee even drew up a complete analysis of it after we had visited it with the office. When we were there, so many different things were happening at the same time: there was a wedding going on, a couple was kissing in a corner, young people were hanging around, tourists were waiting, residents were walking in and out. The fact that a building almost 2,000 years old can still be so lively and absorb such diverse uses touched us deeply. For us, it is the proof *par excellence* that architecture has the power to offer a platform of possibilities and actions that you yourself as an architect cannot imagine. The Castel Sant'Angelo was designed in such a way that it allows all of this. The urge to examine and question everything over and over again is a way for us to stay awake and critical and to see nothing as self-evident. We don't want to develop standard solutions for buildings and then apply them. Because then you'll never obtain the richness that a building like the Castel Sant'Angelo has now.

How do you manage to stay fresh after all these years, to challenge yourselves, while still working on an oeuvre that is growing increasingly consistent?

We really do everything we can to stay awake, to constantly renew ourselves and to let our architecture evolve. At the same time, we're proponents of the long-term process. We've been at it for 20 years now and we really don't feel like it's going to end here. It only gets more exciting, not only because of the larger scale of the projects, but also because of the freedom we have acquired by now. This has to do with the experience in designing and building. We can now really juggle with material atmospheres and a vocabulary that we share with our office. Because most employees stay with us for a longer period of time, we now have a close-knit team with who we share a vision and can really talk. This enables us to conduct experiments and develop proposals that continue to feed our work. It's a particularly pleasant way of working.

So we really can talk of an oeuvre that has acquired a certain self-referentiality and maturity. In the various lines that you have set out, are there any key projects that are game changers, that have set things in motion, that have ushered in a new phase?

The beginning was of course crucial. There were three of us when we started. Joost Verstraete, with whom we founded URA, is therefore not unimportant in our story. That actually grew organically from our student days. We were part of a group of students who were really hungry to work and discover architecture together. In the weekend we would drive to Paris or elsewhere in Europe to see and experience other architecture. At the time, we said that we certainly wouldn't do what we weren't meant to do, i.e. work together as a couple and as best friends. But after our individual internships in different offices, we decided to work together anyway. Because we were aware of the potential dangers, we handled that situation very carefully. We were hungry and always busy with architecture, and so it was natural to start working on a competition design together. The multipurpose hall in Eeklo was the first project. A public assignment at once - which is certainly not self-evident for such a young office! Thanks to this opportunity, we were able to carry out other public projects and further expand our office.

Our way of working means there is now a lot of cross-fertilization between the different projects. Specific themes naturally emerge at some point and are continued later on. For example, the bus station in Bruges actually came into being ten years earlier with our study BXL100, in which we focused on public space and proposed small interventions to make it more exciting and pleasant. That study really contained our way of looking at things and also our belief that you can bring about significant change with small interventions. The seed of the Bruges bus station is therefore in BXL100, but also in a number of art interventions we have done: urban acupuncture, as we call it. That confidence in those smaller elements then also started to play a role in the larger projects.

BXL100

KAU was undoubtedly important, because we were able to convince the client to create more than just a banal gymnasium. And all of these small facets give more baggage to continue working on the next project.

We went through different periods and the way we work changed over time. When Joost left URA, we asked ourselves if we shouldn't just end with a flourish and do something else. We consciously decided at the time to continue as a couple, if only because we didn't really have a choice. We were working on a lot of projects and you can't just terminate them from one day to the next. We continued to work in the same way as if there were three of us, but then just the two of us, and of course by keeping our private and professional lives more clearly separated than ever. But then when we decided to continue the office, it was to go all the way. This has actually only led to an even more intensive involvement with architecture. Undoubtedly the sculptural element came into it more at that time because we were even more involved with architecture as such. The activism of BXL100 receded to the background. It is still part of our projects, but disappeared as an autonomous research in our practice. Today, more than in the past, we focus on pure architectural projects, without the small scale becoming less important for that matter.

You have a reputation for being very likable people, with a special sense of humour. Does that also have a place in your architecture?

The profession of architect has many layers, but above all it is also a serious occupation. Our experience is that you can win a lot of people over through humour. This can be the engineer who spends eight hours a day only doing calculations and whom you take out of his system for a moment by means of humour, or a client you make look at things in a different way.

The story we usually tell is that architecture and building are indeed serious things, but then again, we are all only human and we need to stick together to get the project right. Of course we take our role as architects, in our own way, but we always try to create a kind of convivial atmosphere and, as it were, a community around the project. Humour plays an important role in this. It is a tool by which to discuss many things, to get people out of their comfort zone. It allows us to speak very visually about certain situations so you can relate the staging of the programme to a client to get them into the story as well. Because the client is, of course, a crucial partner for us. It's very important that you get on the same wavelength with the client at some point in order to make the story come true. And this goes for the whole team.

The school in Laeken is a good example. The main building consists of a refectory on the ground floor with classrooms above and the gymnasium at the very top. At one point, Util, the engineering firm, was baffled by our proposal to design the refectory with a construction of steel columns on top of the classrooms on concrete slabs on top of the gymnasium supported by wooden trusses. To them that was a total contradiction in structural terms, but for us that's part of the humour. Sometimes structure has to conform to the best conditions for spatiality and not the other way around. That's a debate we sometimes have with the engineers. But once we get the engineers on board with our way of thinking, it becomes a gripping story for them as well. Humour is a binding agent with which you can turn a design into a collective project. And this holds not only for our view of architecture, but also for our outlook on life.

In addition to an interview, an essay and the project notes, this book also includes a kind of image atlas. What is the status of this collection of images within your architecture practice? Do these collections offer a different perspective on your architecture?

We work with different media, and for each project we decide which medium is best suited to present its ideas in the best possible manner. This ensures a very wide and diverse range of possibilities to show a project. The images in this publication alternate in an intuitively assembled image library. It follows an open structure, with neither a chronology nor a hierarchy.

You can see this collection as a cross-pollination between our mental image library and an iconographic autobiography of our office. It is also related to Aby Warburg's 'Mnemosyne Atlas'. It enables us to bring our projects together in different families and to charge them thematically, but also to discover connections that have long remained implicit. By bringing them together, associative alliances come to the surface, internal relationships between facts that offer room for interpretation. The collection is an accumulation of an aesthetic production in which theory, image and reflection come together and generate an overview of what we call the URA culture.

URA

Biographies

URA Yves Malysse Kiki Verbeeck was founded in 2010 by Yves Malysse and Kiki Verbeeck. They initially launched UR Architecten with Joost Verstraete in 2002. URA Yves Malysse Kiki Verbeeck has been nominated several times for national and international awards, among which the EU Mies Van der Rohe Award, the Bigmat Award and the Belgian Building Award. Malysse and Verbeeck mix practice with research and teaching. They are both guest jurors for several Architecture Schools and Institutions in Belgium and abroad.

Yves Malysse (b. 1973) graduated from the Sint-Lucas Institute of Architecture in Ghent. He has worked with MVRDV in Rotterdam and Jo Crepain in Antwerp, and with stage designer Bart Clement. He was a visiting professor at TU Delft and at the Academy for Architecture in Rotterdam. Since 2012 he has been a professor at LUCA School of Arts, Faculty of Architecture, in Brussels and Ghent.

Kiki Verbeeck (b. 1974) graduated from the Sint-Lucas Institute of Architecture in Ghent and specialized in Architectural Theory at KU Leuven. She has worked in Paris with uapS and Labfac, in Rotterdam with OMA, and in Brussels for Baines and Advisers. She was a guest professor at LUCA School of Arts, Faculty of Architecture Ghent and at KU Leuven, Department of Architecture.

Credits

Projects

BCW
Refectory

Location
Woumen (Diksmuide)

Year
2013–2016

Total floor area
940 m²

Client
Sport Vlaanderen (sports administration of the Flemish government)

DBFM partner
Verstraetebouw

Project team URA
Yves Malysse, Kiki Verbeeck, Wim Dirickx, Michiel van der Loos, Jonathan Robert Maj, Jeroen Kessels

Consultant
Landinzicht

BLB
Bus station

Location
Bruges

Year
2011–2017

Total floor area
8,500 m²

Client
Vlaams Vervoermaatschappij De Lijn (Flemish public transport company)

Project team URA
Yves Malysse, Kiki Verbeeck, Benny Geerinckx, Michiel van der Loos, Alexander Smedts, Wim Dirckx, Jonathan Robert Maj, Adeline de Vrij

Structural engineering
Tractebel

Technical engineering
Tractebel

BTL
Kindergarten and primary school

Location
Laeken (Brussels)

Year
2015–2020

Total floor area
1,800 m²

Client
GO! Onderwijs van de Vlaamse Gemeenschap (Flemish education system)

Project team URA
Yves Malysse, Kiki Verbeeck, Eva Lo, Benny Geerinckx, Isaura Doumen, Jonathan Robert Maj, Harold Vermeiren

Landscape
Landinzicht

Structural engineering
Util

Technical engineering
hp engineers

Consultant
Daidalos-Peutz

BVD
Extension single-family house

Location
Dilbeek

Year
2011–2014

Total floor area
40 m²

Client
private

Project team URA
Yves Malysse, Kiki Verbeeck, Benny Geerinckx, Michiel van der Loos, Sila Griftinoglu, Adeline de Vrij

Structural engineering
Util

DPL
Offices and pavilion

Location
Leuven

Year
2017–2022

Total floor area
3,500 m²

Client
Pleegzorg Vlaams-Brabant en Brussel (Foster care Flemish Brabant and Brussels)

Project team URA
Yves Malysse, Kiki Verbeeck, Eva Lo, Michiel van der Loos, Benny Geerinckx, Tim Belaen, Mathieu Jeukens, Maarten Lambrechts, Charlotte Biesbrouck, Florence Mareen, Felice Van Tieghem, Isaura Doumen

Landscape
Denis Dujardin

Structural engineering
Util

Technical engineering
hp engineers

Consultant
Daidalos-Peutz

HVK
Renovation single-family house

Location
Kemmelberg (Heuvelland)

Year
2011–2015

Total floor area
385 m²

Client
private

Project team URA
Yves Malysse, Kiki Verbeeck, Benny Geerinckx, Alexander Smedts, Mira De Middeleer, Wim Dirickx, Jonathan Robert Maj, Sila Griftinoglu

Landscape
Studio Basta

Structural engineering
Util

JGE
Community spaces

Programme
daycare, housing, polyvalent room, auditorium, social accommodations and common garden

Location
Etterbeek (Brussels)

Year
2015–2020

Total floor area
3,000 m²

Client
City council Etterbeek

Project team URA
Yves Malysse, Kiki Verbeeck, Benny Geerinckx, Mathieu Jeukens, Eva Lo, Jeroen Kessels, Michiel van der Loos, Jonathan Robert Maj, Marius Vaneeckhoutte, Florence Mareen, Isaura Doumen, Anton Parys

Landscape
Landinzicht

Structural engineering
Util

Technical engineering
hp engineers

Consultant
Daidalos-Peutz

JGK
Youth hostel

Location
Kortrijk

Year
2011–2015

Total floor area
2,370 m²

Client
Toerisme Vlaanderen (Tourism Flanders), City council Kortrijk, Province of West Flanders, Howest (Hogeschool West-Vlaanderen)

Project team URA
Yves Malysse, Kiki Verbeeck, Benny Geerinckx, Sofie Lieben, Mira De Middeleer, Pieter Burssens, Wim Dirickx, Alexander Smedts, Mathieu Jeukens, Jonathan Robert Maj, Adeline de Vrij, Jeroen Kessels, Sila Griftinogl

Structural engineering
Snoeck & Partners

Technical engineering
Boydens

Consultant
Landinzicht

KAU
Gymnasium

Location
Uccle (Brussels)

Year
2007–2013

Total floor area
500 m²

Client
GO! Onderwijs van de Vlaamse Gemeenschap (Flemish education system)

Project team URA
Yves Malysse, Kiki Verbeeck, Joost Verstraete, Benny Geerinckx, Wim Dirickx, Frederic Karam, Lorenzo Stroobant, Mathieu Jeukens, Sara Rondou

Structural engineering
Util

Technical engineering
D'Hondt

LWW
Canopy

Location
Watou (Poperinge)

Year
2015–2018

Total floor area
150 m²

Client
City council Poperinge

Project team URA
Yves Malysse, Kiki Verbeeck, Marius Vaneeckhoutte, Jonathan Robert Maj

Structural engineering
Util

PIB
Single-family house

Location
Beigem (Grimbergen)

Year
2009–2013

Total floor area
310 m²

Client
private

Project team URA
Yves Malysse, Kiki Verbeeck, Lorenzo Stroobant, Pieter Burssens, Wim Dirickx, Francis Vanden Bavière, Sofie Lieben, Frederic Karam, Dora Freier, Elena Dragu, Sila Griftinoglu
Structural engineering
Util
Technical engineering
Boydens

RLN
Rehabilitation centre
Location
Ninove
Year
2006–2014
Total floor area
600 m^2
Client
CM Christelijke Mutualiteit Midden-Vlaanderen (health- insurance fund)
Project team URA
Yves Malysse, Kiki Verbeeck, Joost Verstraete, Benny Geerinckx, Lorenzo Stroobant, Frederic Karam, Wim Dirckx, Sara Rondou, Alexander Smedts
Structural engineering
Mouton
Technical engineering
Boydens

SAB
Mixed housing
Programme
student housing, apartments, commercial and social functions
Location
Anderlecht (Brussels)
Year
2017–2024
Total floor area
5,600 m^2
Client
Abattoir and Brik
Project team URA
Yves Malysse, Kiki Verbeeck, Bram Van Sever, Pauline Durand, Mathieu Jeukens, Benny Geerinckx, Jasper Aerts, Florence Mareen
Landscape
Landinzicht
Structural engineering
Util
Technical engineering
Boydens
Consultant
hp engineers (competition)

SPP
Sports facilities
Location
Puurs
Year
2015–2020
Total floor area
1,700 m^2
Client
City council Puurs-Sint-Amands
Project team URA
Yves Malysse, Kiki Verbeeck, Marius Vaneeckhoutte, Benny Geerinckx, Tim Belaen, Charlotte Biesbrouck
Landscape
Buur
Structural engineering
Talboom
Technical engineering
Talboom

TJN
Gymnasium and youth centre
Location
Nazareth
Year
2015–2017
Total floor area
2,000 m^2
Client
City council Nazareth
DBFM partner
Verstraetebouw
Project team URA
Yves Malysse, Kiki Verbeeck, Benny Geerinckx, Eva Lo, Mathieu Jeukens, Wim Dirickx, Harold Vermeiren, Jonathan Robert Maj, Isaura Doumen
Structural engineering
Util
Technical engineering
hp engineers
Consultant
VK engineering

VKW
Community centre
Location
Westrozebeke (Staden)
Year
2015–2019
Total floor area
500 m^2
Client
City council Staden
Project team URA
Yves Malysse, Kiki Verbeeck, Marius Vaneeckhoutte, Benny Geerinckx, Eva Lo, Jonathan Robert Maj, Florence Mareen
Landscape
Landinzicht
Structural engineering
Util
Technical engineering
hp engineers

VOS
Housing
Programme
seven housing blocks with collective platform
Master plan
in collaboration with ectv and advvt
Location
Ghent
Year
2016–2025
Total floor area
22,500 m^2
Client
3D Real Estate
Project team URA
Yves Malysse, Kiki Verbeeck, Michiel van der Loos, Jasper Aerts, Bram Van Sever, Marius Vaneeckhoutte, Jonathan Robert Maj, Charlotte Biesbrouck, Felice Van Tieghem
Landscape
Denis Dujardin
Structural engineering
BM Engineering
Technical engineering
Tractebel
Consultant
Antea Group

WAL
Stacked houses
Programme
three single-family houses
Location
Ledeberg (Ghent)
Year
2010–2015
Total floor area
850 m^2
Client
Oryx
Project team URA
Yves Malysse, Kiki Verbeeck, Pieter Burssens, Wim Dirickx, Lorenzo Stroobant, Benny Geerinckx, Frederic Karam, Sila Griftinoglu
Structural engineering
Nico Terryn
Technical engineering
Istema

WWL
Collective housing
Programme
housing with common areas, conservatoire and crèche
Location
Leuven
Year
2016–2023
Total floor area
17,000 m^2
Client
AGSL Autonoom Gemeentebedrijf Stadsontwikkeling Leuven (city development agency of Leuven)
Project team URA
Yves Malysse, Kiki Verbeeck, Michiel van der Loos, Benny Geerinckx, Eva Lo, Carmen Vandermolen, Pauline Durand, Jonathan Robert Maj, Pauline Truyens, Maarten Lambrechts, Tim Belaen, Ana Horvat, Felice Van Tieghem, Mathieu Jeukens, Lisa Van Com, Isaura Doumen, Egon Pollers
Structural engineering
Tractebel
Technical engineering
Tractebel
Consultants
Denis Dujardin, Tractebel

WZK
Residential care centre
Programme
care centre and service flats with restaurant, offices and grand café
Location
Kortrijk
Year
2010–2017
Total floor area
20,000 m^2
Client
Woonzorggroep GVO Sint-Vincentius (residential healthcare group)
Project team URA
Yves Malysse, Kiki Verbeeck, Wim Dirickx, Michiel van der Loos, Sofie Lieben, Lorenzo Stroobant, Pieter Burssens, Frederic Karam, Mathieu Jeukens, Jonathan Robert Maj, Jeroen Kessels, Mira De Middeleer, Sofie Liesenborghs, Marius Vaneeckhoutte, Sila Griftinoglu, Andrea Neri
Execution architect
Snoeck & Partners
Structural engineering
Snoeck & Partners
Technical engineering
Boydens

Project selection 2002–2020

BKA
Loft interior
Antwerp (B)
2002–2003

DSA
Conversion corner building
Antwerp (B)
2003–2006

LPK
Landscape parking
D'Ieteren
Kortenberg (B)
2004–2006

CTL
Social housing
Lokeren (B)
Competition, 1st prize, built
2005–2014

PZE
Multipurpose hall
Eeklo (B)
Competition, 1st prize, built
2002–2005

AGI
Single-family house
Ypres (B)
2003–2007

THB
Heysel tram terminus
Brussels (B)
Competition, 1st prize, built
2005–2010

RLN
Rehabilitation centre
Ninove (B)
2006–2014

FAR
Single-family house
Rumbeke (B)
2002–2008

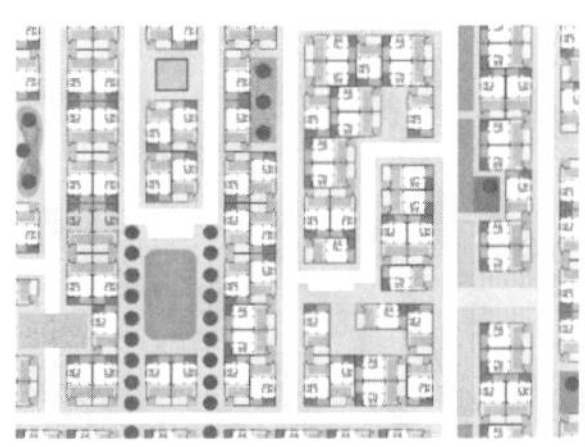

VHM
Ideas competition new
housing types
Competition, 1st prize
2004

GVO
Reception building,
Provincial domain
De Gavers
Harelbeke (B)
Competition, 1st prize, built
2005–2009

KAU
Gymnasium
Uccle (Brussels) (B)
Competition, 2nd prize, built
2007–2013

GAV
Master plan nature and
leisure park Provincial
domain De Gavers
Harelbeke (B)
Competition, 1st prize, built
2003–2017
In collaboration with
Buro Kromwijk,
Landinzicht and ARA

GVZ
Swimming pool pavilion,
Provincial domain
De Gavers
Harelbeke (B)
Competition, 1st prize, built
2004–2009

SJN
Playground Ten Nude
Saint-Josse-ten-Noode
(Brussels) (B)
Competition, 1st prize, built
2005–2008

BXL
Publication BXL 100,
interventions in public space
Brussels (B)
2007–2008

Project selection 2002–2020

35M³
Installation deSingel
Antwerp (B)
2007

KOP
Offices and warehouse
Puurs (B)
2008–2011
In collaboration with Talboom

GOD
Conversion concrete power station
Ghent (B)
Competition, 1st prize
2008

PIB
Single-family house
Beigem (Grimbergen) (B)
2009–2013

XLB
Social housing
Beveren (B)
Competition, 1st prize, built
2007–2016

LPM
Canopy
Mechelen (B)
2008–2012
In collaboration with ARA

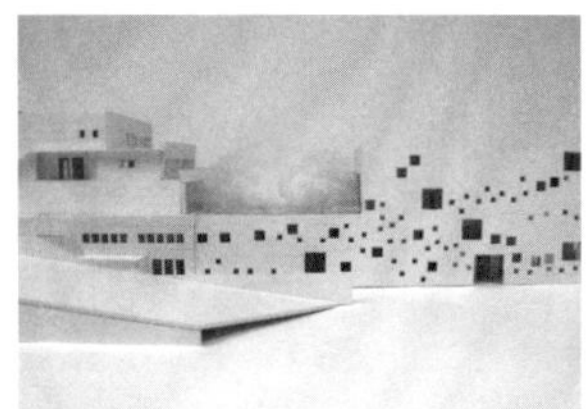

LAC
Extension library Albino
Campobasso (IT)
Competition entry
2009

SLA
Sports and youth centre
Antwerp (B)
Competition, 1st prize
2009

GVW
Watersports building, Provincial domain De Gavers
Harelbeke (B)
Competition, 1st prize, built
2008–2014

LLM
Canopies
Mechelen (B)
2008–2013
In collaboration with ARA

OSB
Bus shelter prototype
Brussels (B)
Competition entry
2009

WAL
Stacked houses
Ghent (B)
2010–2015

ABV
Belgian Pavilion Architecture Biennale Venice
Venice (IT)
Competition entry
2007

JKB
Extension single-family house
Beersel (B)
2008–2012

KWV
Single-family house
Ghent (B)
2009–2012

LL10
Public space installation
Ledeberg (Ghent) (B)
2010–2015

Project selection 2002–2020

KBA
Single-family house
Ghent (B)
2010–2014

BVD
Extension single-family house
Dilbeek (B)
2011–2014

WZE
Residential care centre
Elverdinge (B)
2012–2020
In collaboration with Snoeck & Partners

ACW
Administrative and service centre
Sint-Gillis-Waas (B)
Competition entry
2013

TAH
Secondary technical school
Heist-op-den-Berg (B)
Competition entry
2010

HVK
Renovation single-family house
Kemmelberg (Heuvelland) (B)
2011–2015

SG9
Installation 'Parcours d'artistes'
Saint-Gilles (Brussels) (B)
2012

OAV
Renovation single-family house
Vossem (B)
2013–2016

SWL
Secondary agricultural school
Leuven (B)
Competition entry
2010

JGK
Youth hostel
Kortrijk (B)
Competition, 1st prize, built
2011–2015

HTB
Passenger Port
Brussels (B)
Competition entry
2012

BCW
Refectory
Woumen (B)
Competition, 1st prize, built
2013–2016

WZK
Residential care centre
Kortrijk (B)
2010–2017
In collaboration with Snoeck & Partners

BLB
Bus station
Bruges (B)
2011–2017
Competition, 1st prize, built
In collaboration with Tractebel

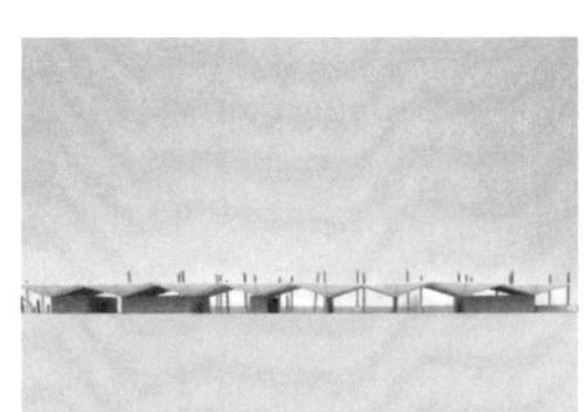

VDB
Warehouses
Brussels (B)
Competition entry
2013

JHU
Two-family house
Uccle (Brussels) (B)
2013–2014

Project selection 2002–2020

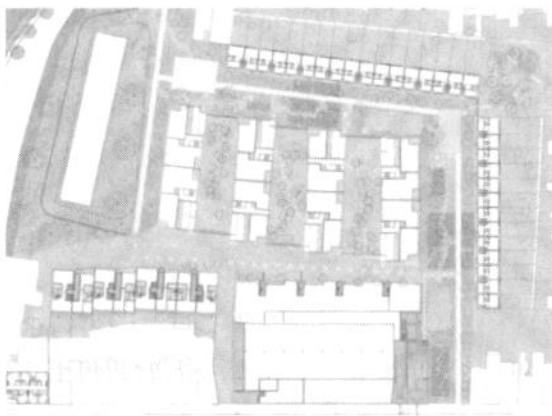

MVZ
Master plan Vaartkom Zuid
Leuven (B)
2013–2019
In collaboration with ectv

WMI
Renovation social housing
Ypres (B)
2014–2021
Master plan by Robbrecht en Daem architecten

LL102
Installation public space
Ledeberg (Ghent) (B)
2015–2021

TJN
Gymnasium and youth centre
Nazareth (B)
Competition, 1st prize, built
2015–2017

BVI
Industrial building
Ingelmunster (B)
Competition, 1st prize
2014

LWW
Canopy
Watou (Poperinge) (B)
Competition, 1st prize, built
2015–2018

GPG
Conversion Military Domain Groenpool
Ghent (B)
2015–2022
In collaboration with Buur

SPP
Sports facilitiy
Puurs (B)
2015–2020
Master plan by Buur

LLB
Extension housing project Léon Lepage
Brussels (B)
2014–2017

GCG
Community centre
Geluwe (B)
Competition entry
2015

BTL
Primary school
Laeken (Brussels) (B)
Competition, 1st prize, in progress
2015–2020

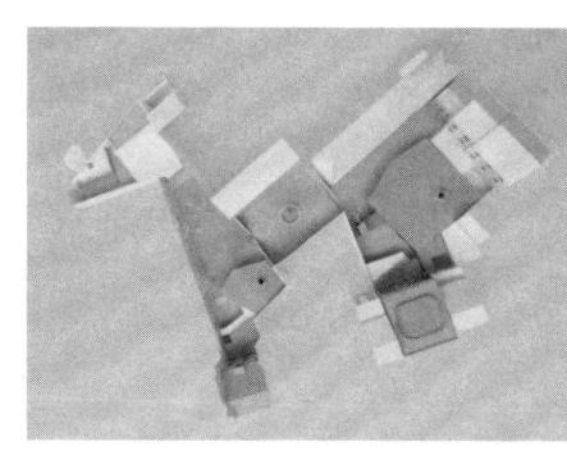

JGE
Community spaces
Etterbeek (Brussels) (B)
Competition, 1st prize, in progress
2015–2021

SSB
Publication
'Students make the city'
Research project for Flemish Government Architect
Brussels (B)
2014–2016

CJG
Cohousing project
Ghent (B)
Competition entry
2015

VKW
Community centre
Westrozebeke (B)
Competition, 1st prize, built
2015–2019

VOS
Housing
Ghent (B)
2016–2025
Competition, 1st prize, in progress, Master plan in collaboration with ectv and advvt

Project selection 2002–2020

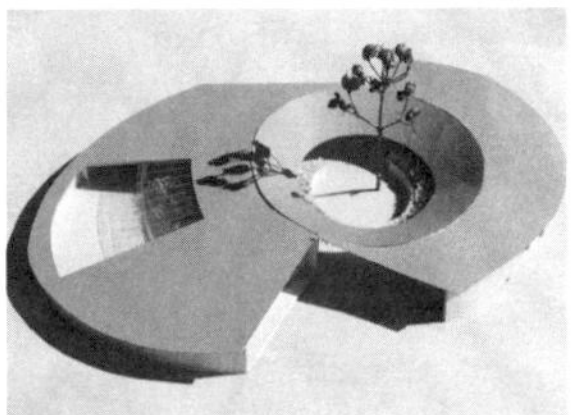

PLM
New public facilities Botanic Garden
Meise (B)
Competition entry
2016

JSB
Renovation town house into office and coworking space
Brussels (B)
2017–2020

WFA
Housing
Antwerp (B)
Competition entry
2018
In collaboration with Robbrecht en Daem architecten

RPZ
Rehabilitation campus Zandhoven (B)
Competition entry
2018
In collaboration with VK Architects

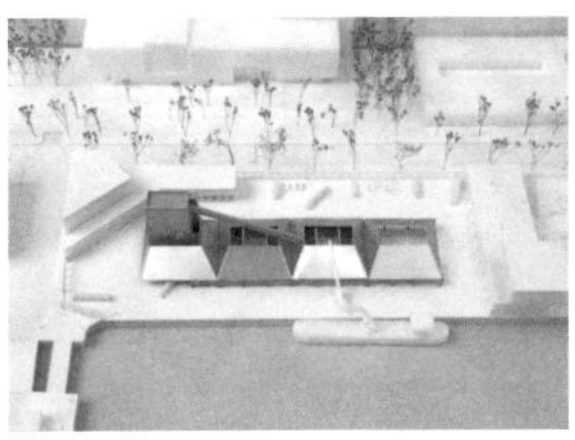

IBB
Reorganization of industrial site
Brussels (B)
Competition entry
2016

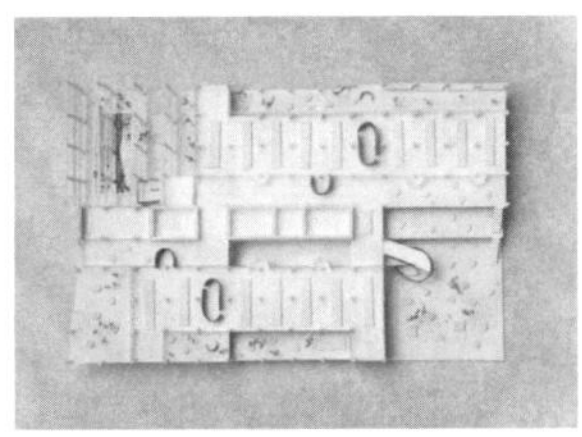

AQA
Campus Aquafin
Aartselaar (B)
Competition entry
2017

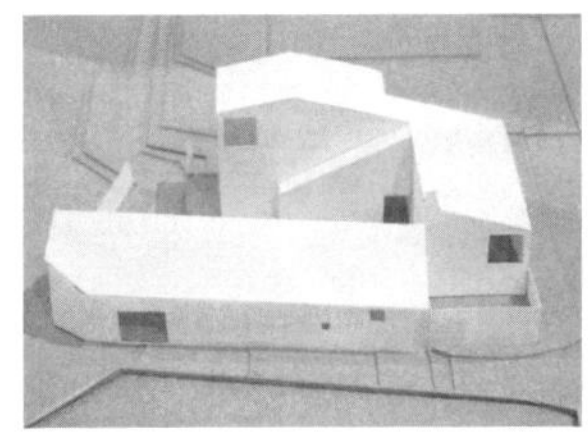

MKL
Collective housing
Leefdaal (B)
2018–2022

BZB
Scenography 'Prints in the Age of Bruegel'
Centre for Fine Arts, BOZAR
Brussels (B)
2018–2019

WWL
Collective housing
Leuven (B)
Competition, 1st prize, in progress
2016–2023

SAB
Mixed housing
Anderlecht (Brussels) (B)
Competition, 1st prize, in progress
2017–2024

BBA
Primary school
Antwerp (B)
Competition, 1st prize, in progress
2018–2022

GWB
Gudule Urban Winery
Brussels (B)
Competition entry
2019

DPL
Office and pavilion
Leuven (B)
Competition, 1st prize, in progress
2017–2022

JDC
House for an artist
Study
2017

BPB
BPost postal centre
Brussels (B)
Competition, 1st prize
2018

MDD
Collective housing
Deinze (B)
2019–2024
In collaboration with Reiulf Ramstad Architects and B2Ai

Colophon

Publication

Concept
Yves Malysse, Kiki Verbeeck

Editors
Lisa De Visscher, Eline Dehullu, Iwan Strauven

Authors
Helen Thomas, Christophe Van Gerrewey, Lisa De Visscher, Iwan Strauven, Eline Dehullu, Francelle Cane, Francis Carpentier

Photography
Filip Dujardin (Projects and Interview), Jeroen Verrecht (Models), URA (Atlas and Project list)

Triptychs
URA Yves Malysse Kiki Verbeeck based on original images by Filip Dujardin

Coordination
Eline Dehullu (A+), Mathieu Jeukens (URA)

Graphic Documents
Mathieu Jeukens, Ana Horvat

English Translation, Copy-editing and Proofreading
Patrick Lennon

Graphic Design and Typesetting
Joris Kritis with Terry Kritis

Publishers
Koenig Books (London), A+ Architecture in Belgium (Brussels), BOZAR Books (Brussels)

Printing and Binding
die Keure (Bruges)

Special thanks to
Joost Verstraete, Benny Geerinckx, Michiel van der Loos, Mathieu Jeukens, Eva Lo, Maarten Lambrechts, Ruth Van de steene, Tim Belaen, Jasper Aerts, Charlotte Biesbrouck, Ana Horvat, Bram Van Sever, Carmen Vandermolen, Pauline Truyens, Sindri Sigurðsson and all former collaborators of URA.

First published by
Koenig Books (London)
Koenig Books Ltd
at the Serpentine Gallery
Kensington Gardens
London W2 3XA
www.koenigbooks.co.uk

ISBN
978-3-96098-834-2

www.ura.be

Distribution

Germany, Austria, Switzerland / Europe
Buchhandlung Walther König
Ehrenstraße 4, 50672 Köln
t.: +49 221 20 59 6 53
verlag@buchhandlungwalther-koenig.de

UK and Ireland
Cornerhouse Publications Ltd. – HOME
2 Tony Wilson Place, Manchester M15 4FN
t.: +44 161 212 3466
publications@cornerhouse.org

Outside Europe
D.A.P. Distributed Art Publishers, Inc.
75 Broad Street, Suite 630, New York, NY 10004
t.: +1 212 627 1999
orders@dapinc.com

This book was published on the occasion of the exhibition *URA – Solid Senses*, held in 2020 at the Centre for Fine Arts Brussels (BOZAR).

Exhibition

Director of Exhibitions
Sophie Lauwers

Managerial Head of Exhibitions
Evelyne Hinque

Senior Curatorial Project Coordinators
Ann Flas, Anne Judong

Architecture Programme
Iwan Strauven

Concept
Yves Malysse, Kiki Verbeeck

Curators
Lisa De Visscher, Iwan Strauven assisted by Lara Molino

Coordination
Lara Molino (A+), Mathieu Jeukens (URA)

Exhibition Design
Yves Malysse, Kiki Verbeeck, Charlotte Biesbrouck, Ana Horvat

Production
Christoph Van Damme

Technical Head of Production
Fred Oulieu assisted by Gert Baart

Lighting
Colin Fincoeur

Assistant to the Director of Exhibitions
Axelle Ancion

Publications Coordinators
Vera Kotaji, Gunther De Wit

Audience Development
Guilliana Venlet

Press
Barbara Porteman

Co-production
Centre for Fine Arts Brussels (BOZAR), A+ Architecture in Belgium

With the support of
Furnibo, Hullebusch, Verstraete.team, Vandersanden, 3D Real Estate, Schüco, Knauf, Tractebel, KU Leuven Faculty of Architecture

Special Thanks:
Charlotte Biesbrouck, Anne Gabriels, Roxane Le Grelle, Steven Palmaers

Centre for Fine Arts Brussels (BOZAR)

CEO – Artistic Director
Paul Dujardin

Financial Director
Jérémie Leroy

Operations Director
Albert Wastiaux

Director of Exhibitons
Sophie Lauwers

Music Director
Ulrich Hauschild

Human Resources Director
Ignace De Breuck

Secretary General
Didier Verboomen

Head of Cinema
Juliette Duret

Head of Artistic Policy Development
Anna Vondracek

Head of Institutional Development
Magdalena Liskova

Head of Marketing & Communication
Sandrine Demolin

Commercial Manager
Luc Préaux

ICT Manager
François Pettiaux

Investments, Security & Archives Manager
Stéphane Vanreppelen

Facility Manager
Guillaume Creusat

Logistics Manager
Rudi Anneessens

Audience Engagement Manager
Tine Van Goethem

Public Services Manager
Matthieu Vanderdonckt

Box Office Manager
Chantal Matthys

Planning Manager
Annik Halmes

A+ Architecture in Belgium

Chair of the Board of Directors
Philémon Wachtelaer

Business Director
Roel Rijssenbeek

Artistic Director
Lisa De Visscher

Deputy Editor-in-Chief
Eline Dehullu

Programme Coordinator
Lara Molino

Production
Grégoire Maus

Office Management
Deborah Schwarzbaum

Communication
Louise Van Laethem

Funding and advertising
Rita Minissi

Triptychs

Symbolen en allegorieën
De natuur en haar symbolen
Het Oude Testament
Heiligen

ONTHAAL